FLOWING, STILL

First published in 2009 by
The Dedalus Press
13 Moyclare Road
Baldoyle
Dublin 13
Ireland

www.dedaluspress.com

ISBN 978 1 906614 04 1 (paper)
ISBN 978 1 906614 05 8 (bound)

Dedalus Press titles are represented in North America
by Syracuse University Press, Inc., 621 Skytop Road,
Suite 110, Syracuse, New York 13244, and in the UK by
Central Books, 99 Wallis Road, London E9 5LN

Cover image © Wild Side Photography / iStockphoto.com

Dedalus Press receives financial assistance from
The Arts Council / An Chomhairle Ealaíon

FLOWING, STILL

Irish Poets on Irish Poetry

Edited by
Pat Boran

DEDALUS PRESS
DUBLIN, IRELAND

ACKNOWLEDGEMENTS

Grateful acknowledgement is made to the editors of the following in which many of these essays, or versions of same, first appeared. (See also notes following the individual essays.)

Watching the River Flow: A Century in Irish Poetry. Eds. Theo Dorgan and Noel Duffy. Poetry Ireland / Éigse Éireann, 1999.

Facing the Music: Irish Poetry in the Twentieth Century. Eamon Grennan. Crieghton University Press, USA, 1999.

Journal of Modern Literature XXV, 1 (Fall 2001).

Poetry Ireland Review, #89, March 2007.

Finding Ireland: a Poet's Explorations of Irish Literature and Culture. Richard Tillinghast. University of Notre Dame Press, 2008.

Contents

TWO

Introduction

Pat Boran

W.B. Yeats and Patrick Kavanagh in the first half of the 20th century, and Seamus Heaney and perhaps a handful of others in our own time, are poets of international standing and importance. They are also often for convenience sake gathered under the heading of 'Irish poetry'. This, however, is difficult to define, because 'Irish poetry' does not neatly fit under a national, or nationalist, banner, is not necessarily made on the island of Ireland, and indeed may not in any direct way concern itself with overtly 'Irish issues'.

The term 'Irish poetry' of course has certain uses, as is noticed and welcomed by Irish poets when they travel abroad. One might argue that the combining of the words 'Irish' and 'poetry' in the magical formula 'Irish poetry' seems to generate a power and strange attraction one does not find in other language cultures. To dismiss this as the result of a crude stereotype or caricature is to underestimate the many in-depth readers who even in the work of the finest and most distinctive Irish poets may feel some sense of a collective voice they would find hard to define. The term 'Irish poetry' will, for instance, often suggest a lyric form, if not a rural then at least an outdoor 'scene' or sensibility, and somewhere close the presence of a sorrow, a sadness, a hurt of some kind that conjures up a past upon which the present seem to tremble as on the surface of a deep lake. (Auden's line to Yeats, "Mad Ireland hurt you into poetry", may be called upon to support this reading, conveniently placing the necessary hurt against a backdrop of madness.

Irish poets continue to be wary of the traps and limitations inherent in a term which might not always allow for complex historical and international connections and influences. There is also the continuing reassessment of 'Irish poetry' by its practitioners in the light of new developments and discoveries the world over: the (English language) influence of Auden and Eliot in the 1930s for instance; of French poets on Denis Devlin and John Montague, among others; the ongoing American connection described here by Eamon Grennan, a Dublin-born poet who, like many Irish poets working in the US—Mary O'Donoghue, Greg Delanty, Sara Berkeley, Gerard Donovan and the late James Liddy among them—is informed by a variety of traditions. And, throughout, the vigour of poetry in the Irish language often acts a touchstone for Irish poets writing in English, many of whom, like Paddy Bushe, the late Michael Hartnett, Gabriel Rosenstock and Gabriel Fitzmaurice, might be said to hold dual passports, translating between the languages, refreshing and challenging the one with the other.

Further complicating the picture are the many non-Irish poets (poets born elsewhere but resident in Ireland—Eva Bourke, Richard Tillinghast and Mark Roper among them) who have long contributed to a living 'Irish poetry' and whose welcome presence expands the meaning of the term.

Writing this introduction just a week after his 70th anniversary (marked in Sligo by a lecture and reading by Seamus Heaney), Yeats is perhaps inevitably on my mind, his obituary in *The New York Times* of January 30, 1939 (available online) painting an odd picture, one whose intention may be fair-minded but which also, more than half a century ago, plays to the stereotype.

"When he labored at his chosen craft, that of writing poetry, essays and plays, Mr. Yeats frequently let his mind roam far afield in the realm of fancy, and it is for the gentle beauty of such works that he was hailed by many as the greatest poet of his time in the English language."

Much, of course, has been written on Yeats, Kavanagh, Heaney and others, and one might argue that it is in part because of the larger conversation which Irish poetry enjoys—and to which many Irish poets themselves contribute—that the term 'Irish poetry' continues to warrant interrogation.

The present volume is, in many ways, a continuation of that interrogation, as it is also a pause in the discussion of generalities and an invitation to refocus on the particulars that are the poet and poems themselves.

WATCHING THE RIVER FLOW

Back in 1999, and no doubt at least in part as a response to the Millennium celebrations then being planned everywhere, Poetry Ireland, the national poetry organisation, under its then Director Theo Dorgan, published the anthology *Watching the River Flow: A Century of Irish Poetry* (edited by Dorgan and Noel Duffy). In it, ten of the major figures in Irish poetry were each given one decade of the 20th century and asked by the editors to choose "ten poems that mark or shape or contain in themselves something of the essential character of that decade".

The resulting volume was one of the most rewarding of recent times, not least for the way in which the concise introductory essays provided a sense of context for the individual poems chosen, even as they also recorded what Eavan Boland called (in her overview of the first decade of that century) the "wonderful cacophony of this moment, its many voices, its multiple purposes".

THE NEW ESSAYS

A decade later, and with that anthology no longer available, the present volume brings back into print those ten introductory essays, as it also sets out to update that volume by including a number of essays which have appeared or been revised since. Between them they show how the river of Irish poetry has continued to flow over the past decade or so. (The idea of reissuing and perhaps adding to those original essays came from Dr. Thomas Dillon Redshaw of the University of St. Thomas in St. Paul, Minnesota who, like many others devoted to the teaching and promotion of Irish poetry, has long bemoaned the absence of a single-volume and affordable prose introduction of this kind.)

The new essays respond, between them, to a variety of poets, certainly more than the 10 allowed to those who surveyed a decade for the original book. History will no doubt whittle this number down in time while voices not yet being heard will emerge. Of course there are, as many of the essayists are at pains to state, other poets and poems which could not be fitted in, but such is the nature of even the most generous editorial policy—if, that is, any significance at all is to attach to the process of selection.

In the second half of the book, then, Theo Dorgan contributes a brief overview of Irish-language poetry; Eamon Grennan considers the rich influence of American Relations on Irish poetry; David Wheatley listens closely to northern voices and telling silences, paying particular attention to the hugely inventive, protean and always risk-taking Ciaran Carson; I myself contribute a shortened version of a talk given at the Yeats Winter School in January 2009 in which I look at responses to the natural world in recent work by poets as diverse as Francis Harvey, Eamon Grennan, Mary Montague, Patrick Deeley and others (more nature trail than thesis, admittedly, a sketch of recent noticings but useful, I hope, as a point of entry—and perhaps the best an editor can hope to provide in such exalted company). To conclude, a welcome presence here, American poet Richard Tillinghast (now resident in

Ireland) gives the salutary outsider's view of a handful of the younger Irish poets who have achieved some prominence in his native land. That these additional essays between them represent almost half of this new volume might be seen as evidence that recent history always requires constant and particularly careful attention. To stay with the metaphor of the flowing river, perhaps the currents always appear fastest moving around one's feet. As not a few of the writers referenced in these essays have yet to receive detailed critical appraisal, at home or abroad, it is hoped that their inclusion here will assist readers interested in seeing where Irish poetry might now be and where it might be going in the coming years.

A number of other first-rate poet-critics might have contributed to this volume, Dennis O'Driscoll, Peter Sirr and Mary O'Donnell among those who come to mind. O'Driscoll's excellent and highly readable *Troubled Thoughts, Majestic Dreams* (Gallery Press, 2001) contains insights on many Irish poets, and his *Stepping Stones: Interviews with Seamus Heaney* (Faber and Faber, 2008) is among the finest of prose volumes on the subject of poetry, Irish or otherwise, in recent times. Mary O'Donnell has produced a good deal of critical writing: her essay 'Irish Women and Writing: An Overview of the Journey from Imagination into Print, 1980-2008' was not available for this book but is included in a forthcoming volume of essays[1] and is recommended as both overview and an account of a personal journey. The probing enthusiasms of Peter Sirr's critical writing have yet to be collected in a prose volume, though a good deal can be found online or in a variety of journals. Eamon Grennan's *Facing the Music: Irish Poetry in the Twentieth Century* (Creighton University Press, 1999) is another significant contribution to the subject, as are Heaney's *Preoccupations: Selected Prose, 1968-1978* (Farrar, Straus, and Giroux, 1980) among other volumes, Eavan Boland's *Object Lessons: The Life of the Women and the Poet in Our Time* (Carcanet Press, 1995) and Gerald Dawe's *The*

---

[1] Writing Bonds. Irish and Galician Contemporary Women Poets. Eds. Manuela Palacios & Laura Lojo. Oxford: Peter Lang, 2009 (forthcoming).

Proper Word: Collected Criticism (Creighton University Press, 2007) to name but three.

As yet there is not a great deal of material in which Irish women poets survey the work of their contemporaries. However, this should not be taken as evidence of any lack of engagement on their part, but it is a regret as I come to finalize this publication. A future companion volume in which Irish poets, both women and men, will respond to the work of a single favourite or influential figure, Irish or otherwise, will, I hope, usefully broaden and add detail to the picture presented here. Poetry by women poets of course features prominently in this book, and one can trace the difficult emergence into print of Irish women poets in the second half of the 20th century (an emergence often evoked for me by the title of Mary Dorcey's 1991 collection, *Moving into the Space Cleared by Our Mothers*). As well as more established figures such as Boland, Paula Meehan, Moya Cannon and Mary O'Malley and others, younger poets such as Sinéad Morrissey, Mary Montague, Áine Ní Ghlinn and Caitríona O'Reilly are just some of the poets whose importance in contemporary Irish writing is rightly reflected in the new material.

Had time and resources been available, I should have liked to see a detailed reading of a number of other poets who do not feature here, among them, for instance, Trevor Joyce, Maurice Scully and Mairead Byrne, poets not working in what might be called the mainstream of Irish writing but who nevertheless contribute to—for the size of its footprint—an astonishingly varied scene. Indeed the richness and variety of contemporary Irish poetry and poetry publishing (one recognises the importance of not just the larger presses but of small imprints such as Summer Palace Press, Bradshaw Books, Doghouse Books, Lapwing Publications and Wild Honey Press, among others) can make it difficult for even the most devoted of readers to keep up. The goal of reissuing and augmenting the original essays from *Watching the River Flow* proved more manageable than the kind of encyclopedia I now find myself wishing for, but which will have to wait for another day.

The "Wonderful Cacophany"

While preparing this volume of essays, the present writer found himself in strong disagreement with the suggestion by Justin Quinn *(The Cambridge Introduction to Modern Irish Poetry, 2008)* that "the disappearance of Ireland" and, by extension, of Irish poetry, may soon be upon us. The selective nature of such works is, as I acknowledge, inevitable and neccesary, but such proclamations seem risible in a book that fails to take account of so many of the most active presences on the contemporary scene— Dermot Bolger, Moya Cannon, Philip Casey, Michael Coady, Tony Curtis, John F. Deane, Katie Donovan, Theo Dorgan, Celia de Freine, Anne-Marie Fyfe, Mark Granier, Francis Harvey, Kerry Hardie, Thomas McCarthy, Gerry Murphy, Mary O'Malley, Paul Perry, Joseph Woods, Macdara Woods and Enda Wyley among them. With only the most superficial glance at what is currently happening, one would find it hard to make any meaningful prediction about the future of Irish poetry.

In contemporary Irish poetry, one might argue that negative response is more likely to come in the form of silence or absence rather than in direct application of any critical apparatus. The question of the dual role of the poet-critic continues to exercise many and is worthy of debate. Dennis O'Driscoll and David Wheatley, among others, have written on the subject. Rather than burden this volume with an overlong introduction, I have posted an essay on one possible strand of this debate on the Dedalus Press blog (http://dedaluspress.blogspot.com/) where the reader may also find links to many of the poets mentioned in the second part of this book.

For this writer, one of the many enrichments rather than limitations offered by the term 'Irish poetry' is the way in which it brings into proximity the work of writers as diverse as Dermot Healy, Vona Groarke, Eamonn Wall and Nuala Ní Dhomhnaill, Derek Mahon, Paul Muldoon, Paula Meehan and Maurice Riordan, none of whom seem in the slightest degree confined by the efforts of their fellows, and all of whom engage with and enrich the history and traditions that continue to effect them as citizens, as readers and as writers, whatever their current geographic, historical or formal interests. The essays gathered, and re-gathered, in this volume will, I hope, serve as an introduction to what Theo Dorgan (quoting Yeats) called in his Introduction to *Watching the River Flow* "the living stream"—from whose banks today the waters look as energetic as ever.

Lá Fhéile Bríde
01 February 2009

ONE

Introductory essays from
*Watching the River Flow:
A Century in Irish Poetry* (1999)

Beginnings (1900—1909)

Eavan Boland

I wish I could re-construct the life, the circumstances, the hopes of an Irish poet in 1900. But it is impossible. The difficulty comes from the fact that we have kept the poems but lost their hinterland. That back country of talk, noise, bitterness, faction and magical self-discovery matters to these poems more than a context usually matters to a text. For want of those passionate voices, I am going to try to make some place for these ten poems that suggests their existence at the edge of a whirlwind. But I have those lost voices in my mind as well. And so I have chosen these poems very deliberately to try to recover some of the untidy, hard-to-define energy of that decade.

1900 seemed, on the surface anyway, to offer a peaceful prospect in Ireland. It was, of course, deceptive. Two nations existed, two visions of Ireland were in play. A small catalogue of the year's events is sufficient to list the contradictions: in January of that year the members of the Parnell memorial committee met in the Mansion House to report a collection of six thousand pounds for his memorial; in April Queen Victoria arrived for a three week visit; in December Maud Gonne got the freedom of Limerick city. But in December, as if to remind everyone of the neighbourly necessities, the City of Dublin Steampacket Company announced four Royal Mail Steamers to travel between Dublin and Holyhead in the faster time of three hours.

"What constitutes an Irish poet?" asked Donagh MacDonagh in his introduction to the 1959 *Oxford Book of Irish Verse*. In the first years of the century, the question had a new edge and force. Not just Irish poetry, but Irishness itself was changing rapidly. It was not only Miss Ivors who was scolding Gabriel Conroy about taking his holidays in Ireland. The argument was universal. But what argument? The answer to that is more elusive. These poems with their many images, their mirrors of rhetoric are small maps of a country in crisis. From now on to be Irish, to know it, to write it, to state it, will be on occasions, and literally, a matter of life and death. Tom MacDonagh's poem seems to have a premonition of it. But to be Irish, in this decade especially, may also mean exile, complicated distance, volatile rejection. But enough. The best way of illustrating this unique time of quicksand and change in Irish poetry is by talking about the poems and the poets.

"Suddenly in 1900," wrote Yeats, "everybody got down from their stilts. Nobody drank absinthe anymore with his black coffee." But Yeats wrote that many years later, thinking back to a time when his influences were as much French and British as Irish. The grace of retrospect is a late-comer however. Up close it was different. For him this decade was a time of fire, bitterness, abrasion, ordeal. Synge died. The nationalists moved sharply away from him and rioted in his theatre. His diaries show the strain of every conversation and quarrel that brought him up against the coming estrangements of history. 'The Mask', later published along with 'No Second Troy' in *The Green Helmet*, draws me in because of its surreal tensions, its new command—derived from drama—of tone and transition. This may not be the most demanding or challenging poem he wrote in this decade. Nevertheless, it is hard to find one that shows more thoroughly his mastery of the abrupt lyric drama.

The early years of the century provided plenty of static for anyone living in Ireland. In the first few years, newspapers reported a set of contradictions. Everywhere illusion and contrast were the order of the day. But below these surfaces, energies and influences ran into Irish poetry which it would take more time and far more pain to get rid of. One of the events of this decade was the publication of Padraic Colum's *Wild Earth*. He was in his middle twenties when the book came out in 1906. There is no doubt, looking back, that its complex portrait of a pastoral Ireland is deeply flawed. Colum's constituency was just too far apart from his readership for it to be otherwise. For all that, the poem here, 'A Poor Scholar of the Forties', is one of the remarkable pieces in a book which marked out a new subject matter, if not a new politic. The poem is powerful. How could it not be? The tragedy of language, the fracture of identity cracks open ornament and rhetoric and suddenly the world of Mangan shows its dark, lost face for a moment, and is gone again.

A time of trams and uniforms, of broken Parliamentary promises and exciting theatre nights. The young man—eleven years older than Colum and six years younger than Yeats—who wrote 'To the Oaks of Glencree' now seems a very distant figure. John Millington Synge is a casualty of the time. Dying from throat cancer in his thirties, wounded by the *Playboy* riots, this short, dark poem may reveal his fears. It is also elegant, awkward, haunting. This is the voice that should be paired with another young man in his thirties, Thomas MacDonagh, to provide mirror images— twinned and contrasted—of the young Irish poet. Of course MacDonagh and Synge both had other compelling identities. But for that very reason they are comparable. This may have been the last decade in Ireland and Irish poetry before a real narrowing. All kinds of voices are coming in, all kinds of layering is going on. Before the nation, before the violence, before the demands for consistency which a national literature inevitably imposes, we can enjoy this young Wicklow dramatist talking to the beautiful unharmed oaks of his region. And turn around, almost at once, and listen to Thomas MacDonagh— another world, another country, a different purpose—predicting and defining the world of the poet patriot.

In 1910 the Phoenix publishing house in Dublin published *Songs of the Irish Rebels and Specimens from an Irish Anthology* by Padraic Pearse. The poems in this volume, according to Pearse's footnotes, were mostly published between 1900 and 1907 in *An*

Claidheamh Soluis. 'The Stars Stand Up' is typical in its force and unapologetic rhetoric. In fact the whole text of the book is scattered and brightened by Pearse's comments—idiosyncratic, wayward, unpredictable. Something about what makes this decade so endearing in Irish poetry is shown by the fact that Pearse's faithfulness to the dream of a free and Gaelic Ireland can co-exist with a tender-heartedness for the less faithful: Pearce Ferriter, he says, "was a poet of very versatile culture: his love and satirical poems have the grace and deftness of Moore." The wit and grace of Pearse—qualities somehow overlaid in the later silhouette of the leader of the 1916 Rebellion—as well as the fluidity of the time are somehow most clearly shown in this unswerving patriot remarking companionably about one of the most eel-like navigators of the nineteenth century.

I like this fragmented, all-over-the-place moment. I like the way the nation is near enough to be a purpose, a dream, a theme, but not so near that it becomes a template. I like the fact that Yeats's masks and Pearse's stars can draw on the same oxygen as MacDonagh's patriot poet and Colum's heartbroken scholar. This is a decade defined by what has not happened as much as by what has: the nation has not defined itself. Modernism, stirring in Paris and New York and London, has not yet come to the edges of the Irish poem. History—of art, of Ireland—is in abeyance.

What I don't like, and I have wanted to avoid, is any attempt to re-write this untidy, rich, complicated moment in our history and our poetry with the symmetry of our retrospect and our later self-definition. With this in mind, as well as for other reasons, I have included the powerful witness of four women poets here. Steadily, incrementally, their work was edited out of the anthologies from the fifties to the present day. Yet this falsifies a time in which they were a vivid, compelling presence. Not always a polite one either. At least one, Susan Mitchell, is included for the sharp and funny air of her language, and the way her briskly managed satire reminds us that this was a decade of robust exchange as well as lyric rhetoric. Another poet, Ethna Carbery, never lived to see the decade, but was published in it. Katharine Tynan went on to bring out many volumes while Dora Sigerson Shorter had been publishing for years.

There is no doubt that the rhetoric in these poems of the nation, of the woman, is at times stilted. I have certainly resisted that in other writing, and I question it just as much here as well. But it is poignant and essential to listen to these poets. They come into this decade speaking the language of 1848, talking with the music and extravagance of the nineteenth century. But Ethna Carbery, Dora Sigerson Shorter, and Katharine Tynan were also about something much more serious. They were trying out the first hesitancies and images of Irish women. They may be daughters of Speranza and Lady Morgan. But they were also fascinating voices, not least because they point to the future in the language of the past. Without them the record of this decade in Irish poetry, with its decorous language covering dark uncertainties, is incomplete.

The story of Ethna Carbery is somehow emblematic of this time. Dying two years before the century began, her voice lasted well into it. *The Four Winds of Eirinn* was published in 1906 by M.H. Gill together with Jas. Duffy and Co. Ltd. The elaborate bookplate of later editions announces that the poems have sold more than ten thousand copies. It makes a valuable counterpoint to *Wild Earth* by Padraic Colum: both seeking out a rhetoric and a subject matter which is not yet separable from the audience which expects and demands a meaning as well as a music. Both rehearsing, in a profoundly touching way, problems later Irish poets like Kavanagh would set out to resolve with an energy matched only by anger.

This is a decade of surprises, contradictions, unsettled surfaces in Irish poetry. There is no danger in that. The danger is that, in retrospect, we might try to smooth it out, with a set of importances and a pattern of selection which denies the wonderful cacophony of this moment, its many voices, its multiple purposes. Praise to the end. This has been, in many ways, the Irish century in poetry. But here in its sprawling beginnings is a family history like any other: colourful, embarrassing, and greatly to be cherished.

Changes & Translations (1910—1919)

EILÉAN NÍ CHUILLEANÁIN

The second decade was the one that set the tone for the kind of century it was to be, for the world and for Ireland. It was a period of dreadful war in Europe and beyond, of great national and social antagonism, of enormous change. And since for once we are invited to generalise, it was the decade in which the impossible began to seem possible, even such impossibilities as women elected to parliaments, as the rebirth of Gaelic culture, as an end to seven and a half centuries of British rule in Ireland. A poem by Stephen Gwynn, included in my school anthology of the 1950s, seemed not to earn its passage in the present collection, but it came back to me when I started to think of my choices. It was called 'A Song of Defeat' and it went back to the last time the Irish had won a war, in 1014. I remember the lines: "Brian fought and he fell/ But Brian fought and he won; / God that was long ago!" By 1919 the mournful litany of past defeats and exiles no longer seemed to sound the essential Celtic note, endlessly elegiac.

The poetry of these ten years sometimes appears merely to register the shock of crucial events, most memorably in Yeats's 'Easter 1916' with the starkness of its "all changed, changed utterly," and the acceptance that poetry must now assimilate new, contemporary names, "I write it out in a verse/ MacDonagh and MacBride/ and Connolly and Pearse …". It reminds me of Milton's

22

rejection of the names that "would have made Quintilian stare and gasp", "Colkitto and MacDonald and Galasp" in his sonnet on names, 'A book was writ of late call'd *Tetrachordan*'. If Yeats was echoing Milton he was marking an acceptance of what Milton's Graeco-Latinity had graded as dross, a divergence out of the main street, Milton's street, of a metropolitan culture into a national literature where the poet himself was to acquire a new name, "I, the poet, William Yeats," as he was to call himself in a verse, 'To be carved on a Stone at Thoor Ballylee' in *Michael Robartes and the Dancer.*

Yeats, as he knew and we know, was in part confronting the unexpected countenance of something he had helped to make himself, in part appropriating the work of others, in part defining his own role in a new Ireland; and after all not quite abandoning his place as a poet of the English-speaking world who published in London and consorted with English Duchesses. But a public voice came to him in this decade of Ireland's revolution and of his own marriage and the end of his long fantasy about Maud Gonne, and it came after he rejected another role, that of war poet. His refusal 'On being asked for a war poem' was lofty and wilful: "I think it better that in times like these / A poet's voice be silent …" since "He has had enough of rhyming that can please / A young girl in the indolence of youth". It was a different story when he had to respond to the actuality of the war in Ireland.

Yeats's work in this period, in *Responsibilities, The Wild Swans at Coole,* and including the poems in *The Tower* written before 1920, contains so much excellent poetry as to have made a choice difficult. I hesitated over many celebrated pieces, especially the poems on the controversy about the Hugh Lane collection and the death in action of Robert Gregory, I considered songs from plays, including the splendid 'Musicians' Song' beginning "Come to me, human faces" from *At the Hawk's Well,* and ended by choosing a poem I have loved since I was a child, suggesting that the lofty and wilful side of Yeats had not disappeared entirely with the advent of new responsibilities. Like so much of his early work it has a fragile music; reading it now one seems to hear a draft of a translation from another language, an attempt to capture a rhythm and an idiom that indeed seems for a moment to illuminate English with its reflected gleam, or to offer a medium for looking at the world through like the hare's collar-bone.

Translation from the Irish had by the beginning of the century changed its role. It was no longer a matter of conveying a version of Irish literature for the benefit of English-speaking monoglots; enough readers of Irish existed to be able to judge the translator's performance, fidelity and creativity, as eighteenth-century English readers could judge Pope's version of Homer. Yeats's pastiche of a language he did not understand works like music, alludes to music and plays on a single strain that exists in the Gaelic tradition, the otherworldliness that he had first exploited in *The Wanderings of Oisin* and *The Land of Heart's Desire*. The work of true translation is to create a recognisable substitute for a known original. Much of Gaelic poetry is not evanescent or otherworldly at all, and it was the hardness, even harshness, of a love-poem from the Gaelic, Colum's 'O woman, shapely as a swan' that surprised G.K. Chesterton when he published it in a collection of new poems in 1910. The loud assertiveness of James Stephens's 'O'Bruadair', the metrical energy of MacDonagh's version of 'An Bunnán Buí', both published in 1916, do not surprise but delight the reader who knows these poets. The Gaelic scholarship and the publishing which produced among much else T.F. Ó Rathaille's edition of *Dánta Grádha*, Enrí Ó Muirgheasa's of *Céad de Cheoltaibh Ulaidh* and the work of the Irish Texts Society (which supplied the immediate source texts for Colum, MacDonagh and Stephens) had created an audience with the critical awareness needed to recognise these poems as among the finest of the decade, and also to notice the often quite striking divergence from the originals. Colum's line in his last stanza, "In a cunning house hard-reared was I" has a rueful plangency missing from the original *Dánta Grádha*. Stephens characterises his own work as "Loot, or plunder" rather than translation, qualifying this in the case of Ó Bruadair as "almost... translation of one side of his terrific muse."

Stephens's encounters with the poet whose voice he describes as "an unending rebellious bawl which would be the most desolating utterance ever made by man if it were not also the most gleeful" gives us a historical moment sharply recaptured, a singular embattled poetic talent reflected by a different, much gentler one. Padraic Pearse's 'Mise Éire' is not a translation but an allusion to the whole of a millennial tradition in Gaelic, reaching back far beyond Ó Bruadair. Its use of the personification trope so widely elaborated in Gaelic poetry is striking here in its verbal simplicity: Ireland as goddess, as Cailleach, as mother, revealed in two words, and the twentieth-century speaker's claim to speak for historical Ireland as outspoken as it was to be two years later, in the immediacy of English, in the 1916 Proclamation of the Republic. The clarity of the poem, the stillness, vibrates with expectation, the first person "Mise" is the claim to speak in the present, thus to proclaim that Ireland's history is not at an end.

If Yeats had refused the role of war poet until it was forced on him by Pearse's other war, there were a number of Irish poets, not particularly loyalist in sentiment, who responded to the Great War of the decade as to an inevitable theme. Francis Ledwidge was killed in the war, and a number of his poems were written on active service. I thought of including 'The sheep are coming home in Greece' for its sharpness of observation, or one of the better-known pieces in which he juxtaposes the experience of war and his thoughts of home. But a poem that has nothing to do with the war, 'The Wife of Llew', seduced me with its directly sensuous approach to myth. For a war poem I had to turn to Katharine Tynan's mysterious and shadowy view (not her only handling of the subject; she was extremely, even awfully, prolific during the war years) of the deaths of young men as of a piece with their growing up and leaving home.

Tynan's is also a religious view, as so often in her work. This was a period when religious verse, mystical or pious, was written in quantity, when the reputation especially of the lately dead Francis Thompson was influential in many quarters, when Ireland as a country where religion was very important might have expected to produce a Hopkins or a Blake. But it didn't happen. The despairing expression of faith in the last line of Tynan's poem is touching and doesn't distract from the central emptiness of the bereaved lives the poem describes. More truly *about* human ideas about God and destiny is Æ's 'Icicles' with its cold evolutionary view of the "Death of God". There is perhaps suppressed debate going on between these two poems. Their faith or mysticism confronts a void, or an absence, profoundly distracting questions of a kind whose presence in Irish poetry, since they are not the kind of individualist issues that touched Yeats or Joyce, later critics tend to ignore.

The political and the mystical do however remain close throughout this decade. Perhaps because of this, the lyric with its characteristic intensity seemed the essential form of poetry in English. Translation offered an occasional relief from such concentration; so did comic verse such as Susan Mitchell's, Tom Kettle's, or Eimhar O'Duffy's, none of which I have been able to find room for. Joseph Campbell's collection *Irishry* is not a comic volume but in its attempt to include a wide variety of Irish types it looks away from the lyric to irony and energy. I have included the poem on an Irish newspaper seller in New York as a reminder that it was possible to look at class, to include urban and small-town experience and to use different narrative styles in the poetry of this decade, the last before Campbell too was to emigrate to America, like Padraic Colum and like so many of the citizens of the new State. Both were to continue to write, but their exiles meant a diminishing of their relationship to the Irish material rather than an empowering distance like Joyce's. For many Irish poets the events of the decade brought an ending. Pearse, MacDonagh and Ledwidge died in different wars. Stephens still had plenty to say, but in prose. Only Yeats was to write some of his finest poetry in the 1920s and 30s; with war and the foundation of a new state the very meaning of poetry too had changed utterly.

"Who Speaks for These?" (1920—1929)

BERNARD O'DONOGHUE

No period promised as much change, politically and culturally, in Ireland as the early 1920s: the end of rule from London and of the First World War; the socially defining watershed of the Civil War; the development of the cultural and linguistic changes initiated by the Gaelic League and the Celtic Revival. More widely there was the changing European world marked by Modernism: 1921 was the year of *The Waste Land*. But, according to the conventional accounts, the excitement of the promise of diversification in all this gradually faded, and the decade ended with the narrowing of horizons eloquently and depressingly expressed in the new State's censorship laws. Yeats's Senate speeches, most notably on divorce, are taken as the death-knell of pluralism.

It is increasingly being seen though that this is too simple an account, principally because cultural and political progress are by no means invariably in step. Indeed there is no period which bears this discrepancy out so strikingly as the high point of Modernism in the 1920s when the cultural avant-garde in Europe was often inextricable from the politically unenlightened. One of the oddest phenomena in literary criticism in our time is the increasingly desperate attempts by the critical mainstream to argue that T.S. Eliot couldn't have been reactionary because *The Waste Land* was groundbreaking. The world after the end of The Great War was not a simple one.

And there is no simple one-for-one artistic-historical correspondence in Ireland either, though the traditional literary-historical narratives often provide one. Ireland did have its own distinctive problems, it is true. New states face problems of definition. The Irish version of this problem was put most famously by Daniel Corkery in 1934 when, in his much-decried book *Synge and Anglo-Irish Literature*, he surveyed the attenders at a Munster Hurling Final in Thurles and asked "Who speaks for these?" It is a good question for the writer, and one susceptible of a wider interpretation than it has often been given. The new state, in cultural terms, had a complex and divided inheritance, a complexity which is readily evident in the poetry of the 1920s. It was a great deal more intricate than the post-factum binary division that has usually been made: on the one hand Yeatsian Celtic Twilight conservative; on the other an overpowered enlightenment struggling gallantly towards modernity in reaction against that and other atavisms.

The complexity is well illustrated in Yeats's own poetry. 'Meditations in Time of Civil War' finds "no clear fact to be discerned". No poem of its period, anywhere in Europe, voices our own concerns in terms more sympathetic to our day. It bears as crucially on 1990s Yugoslavia as on Ireland in 1923:

> We had fed the heart on fantasies,
> The heart's grown brutal from the fare;
> More substance in our enmities
> Than in our love.

Yeats, after the Nobel Prize in 1923, was often thought a stiflingly dominant presence. This view of Yeats as the force to be resisted has damaged the reputation of Austin Clarke more than any of the followers of the master. Everyone admires the lyrical charms of 'The Planter's Daughter'; yet the prevailing view of the "Celtic-Romanesque" Clarke has prevented us from seeing the poem's bearing on the new Ireland. Clarke reminds us that, in aesthetic terms, the privileges of the Planter class brought with them enviable graces. Men and women of all classes are excited by the daughter's beauty: "And O she was the Sunday/ In every week". Clarke has been thought narrow because of his insistent addressing of Corkery's question about the literary constituency; but his answer to it is at least as challenging historically as that of the Modernists who left Ireland in order to contemplate the problem at a distance. To put it glibly, if the moral of 'The Planter's Daughter' had been properly taken, no great house would have been burned.

'The Planter's Daughter' also exemplifies another major strand in the Irish poetic inheritance. The inspirational "O" in the first of the lines I have just quoted is necessary to meet the metrical demands of the seven-syllable line of Old Irish poetry, also reflected in the assonantal pattern in "fire", "night", "crowd", "proud". There were other attractive ways of linking to the Gaelic past which the poets of the 20s explored; Frank O'Connor gave a voice (and a highly romantic title) to Aodhagán Ó Rathaille's bitter 'Vailintín Brún', but he borrowed its musical voice too in 'A Grey Eye Weeping'. And more directly the 1920s saw the accelerated origins of lyric poetry in Irish that was to yield such fruits in the later generations of Ó Direáin, Ó Ríordáin and Mhac an tSaoi, and later again in Ní Dhomhnaill and Ó Muirthile. What is striking in looking at the lyrics of Séamas Ó hAodha or Liam S. Gógan is the confidence which characterizes the relatively new form in Irish. The sheer metaphorical style and verbal wit of 'An Ghaedhilg' ('To Irish') is hard to match in 1920s poems in English.

Gógan also represented the urban in Irish poetry. Its expression in English is most associated with Joyce's prose (the everyday of the city is almost entirely absent from his poetry, apart from the famous 'Cabra') but the city is prominent in 20s poets too. Joyce's friend and enemy Oliver St John Gogarty was energetically opposed to the bucolics of the Celtic Revival. Although his poetry has limitations, he is an important presence for two reasons: first, his classically-correct forms are an explicit reaction to the view of the Celtic world as misty and sentimental (though by now that reaction—the postulate of the hard-headed

Celt—has become almost as much of a stereotype as the Arnoldian imaginative Celt it opposes); secondly, Gogarty is significant for the more sustained presence in his poetry of the satirizing of the Celtic Revival most famously featured in Joyce's 'Gas from a Burner'. In this mode Gogarty was the last representative of a distinguished group which included Synge and Stephens as well as Joyce. But he also harks forward to a classicism associated with Northern and Trinity College writers such as Derek Mahon.

There were other anticipatory voices. Blanaid Salkeld's *Hello Eternity!* was admired by Beckett not for its "blue in the face" sonnets, but for its modern sensibility. Her later volume *The Fox's Covert* (1935) anticipates remarkably much of the women's poetry written in post-1960s Ireland, if not indeed the more radical tones of radical French feminism:

> From the cold and wise merman I have concealed well,
> Motherly wise.

But the roots of that radicalism are already evident in the strangeness and ironies of 'Invitation'. Besides, Salkeld's social and geographical history is exemplary for the diaspora that was to feature so much in Irish writing in the new century; she was born in Pakistan and, after an Irish childhood, married an English civil servant and briefly lived in Bombay in the twilight of the Raj. After her husband's early death, she returned to Ireland at the age of twenty-eight and remained there, writing as a classic "internal exile", in both social and sexual terms.

The early era of the new State is often presented as a failure to tune in to Modernism. Again, traditional accounts straighten things out too neatly. The names usually invoked are Beckett, Devlin, Coffey and MacGreevy, as poets who gave up on Irish Modernism as a bad job or a contradiction in terms. At the end of the century when we are anxious to revise reputations, Coffey and Devlin have remained obdurately hard to revive and Beckett is supranational. MacGreevy now looks the most interesting case of a

1920s (and after) Modernist Irish poet: a Ledwidge who survived the Trenches to become a modern European poet of Irish experience. In choosing his 'Homage to Jack Yeats', I am thinking too of its original title 'Dysert' which acts as a reminder that an Irish placing could be transplanted into the mixed Modernist form MacGreevy derived from Eliot. More than any other poet MacGreevy brought the Irish experience—including the trauma of civil war—into a perspective that belongs to the same world as the Spanish Civil War.

In the twentieth century as a whole, of course, the poets who most invite comparison with the War Poets of the Trenches or of the Spanish Civil War are the Northern Troubles poets of the 60s: Montague, Heaney, Simmons, Longley and others. By contrast, the northern voices are oddly silent in the 1920s, at least as a distinct group. It may be that a distinctive northern voice, either linked to or contrasted to the new State, was yet to emerge; two of its great figures, MacNeice and Hewitt, are about to appear, just as the great rural poet Kavanagh is about to mould a new kind of writing in the south. Strangely, the Meath Protestant F.R. Higgins manages to anticipate both constituencies in a way: in 'Father and Son', the father—"that proud, wayward man"—is unmistakably Anglo-Irish while standing at the crossroads to the new rural world. That world, which was to be hideously evoked in Kavanagh's 'The Great Hunger', was founded on an uneasy pastoral of which Padraic Colum's poems (such as 'A Drover') were memorable examples. Colum's later poems (none of his successful poems was very late) such as 'Song of Starlings' here have a new socio-psychological edge to them. Like 'A Drover', these poems in *Old Pastures* (1930) are strikingly prophetic of the uncertainty with the new order, an uncertainty which in a different way is also evident in the over-protesting of de Valera's vision of the ideal community which it was hoped would follow from the Economic War. Finally, a poet who might be linked with Colum (as Joseph Campbell of the previous decade often has been) is Seumas O'Sullivan, an enabler of other writers. I will end with him as a figure of the pluralist complexity that is often said to be lost in the more single-stranded Ireland that is imputed from the start of the 1930s. A late O'Sullivan poem like 'The Lamplighter' both in its title and its subject anticipates Thomas Kinsella. It represents the necessary—and perhaps reluctant—movement from the Irish bucolics of earlier O'Sullivan poems in *The Earth Lover* (1909) to the harsher business of the new State's politics: the recognition of Yeats's Parnell that "Ireland shall get her freedom and you still break stone."

This was perhaps the summary moral of 1920s Irish poetry, as indeed of the worldwide ideological feeling of that decade when the ideal of "homes fit for heroes" at the end of The Great War gave way to a much harsher political order. And as Yeats lives on, to dominate his last decade more absolutely than any previous one, his politics too became more embittered and more uncertain.

The Nineteen Thirties (1930—1939)

Thomas Kinsella

Yeats remained creatively active in the 1930s, in his seventies, with an art adequate to all his demands. His last poems, profound and wide in range, include considerations of the meaning of human life, accepting and defining its limitations. In 'The Choice', the choice is one of dedication: to worldly success or to the quality of the work, one excluding the other. We might question the necessity of this, in view of Yeats's apparent success in managing both. But we do not have Yeats's own certain assessment of his life's achievement. The evidence varies. It appears generally favourable, but the evidence in this poem is that in dedicating himself to the work Yeats believes he has foregone something important in life. Dedicated to art, and marked with toil, he is ending his life with feelings of inadequacy and dissatisfaction. In 'What Then?' the conclusion is the same. A life of purposeful toil is coming to an end, with only the toil certain. 'Under Ben Bulben', Yeats's dramatic exit, provides a possible resolution. Nothing remains for the individual, but with "Something to perfection brought" the individual contributes toward an overall human achievement, "Profane perfection of mankind", with art in the place of religion, as in 'Sailing to Byzantium'. The poem, at this point at its most profound, settles into stage Irish with Yeats's directions to Irish poets, and ends in rhetoric—considering the difficulties in the way of reading an epitaph in Drumcliff churchyard, however memorable, from horseback.

At the time of Yeats's death Austin Clarke was in his early forties. Some of the poems in *Night and Morning,* published in 1938, are clear and eloquent. 'Her Voice Could Not Be Softer' presents with quiet sensuousness a woman in the act of love, and the intrusion—equally sensuous—of the dominant Catholicism of the time. Other poems are in the difficult and eccentric manner of his middle career, as in 'Tenebrae'. This rejects the requirements of Catholicism direct, the poet in the throes of refusal, in doubt and pride, an agonised Luther.

The material of Patrick Kavanagh's career was based on a primitive inner certainty. But a great deal of his poetry is negative; angry at the intellectual and artistic Ireland of his time; uneasy, knowing he has no place in it; and critical of its inadequacies. In two poems from the early 1930s this material is already in place. In the negative 'Dark Ireland' a selfishness in the Irish soul stands between contemporary Ireland and the truth of things. In the positive 'Tinker's Wife', the truth is in the facts, presented directly to the poet. He records them and communicates them directly, without the interference of literature.

The poetry of Clarke and Kavanagh in the 1930s is written in an enclosed Ireland, a religious and post-colonial dead end, with no significant outside contacts. Other Irish poets of the time were at home in an outside world. Samuel Beckett was at home also in the new poetics, in poems that nobody read, or reads. He wrote 'Cascando' in early love (in his thirtieth year) to a visitor from Boston. It is directed inward as much as toward the beloved, and she failed to understand, or respond.

Louis MacNeice, least "Irish" of Irish poets, was at home in an English poetic tradition. He wrote in the 1930s in the powerful influence of W. H. Auden. Both poets were inclined toward intellectual entertainment, but they were aware of the growing seriousness of things in Europe in the late 1930s. For a little while still it was possible to pretend, and play adult games. MacNeice and Auden, to write a travel book, went to Iceland. *Letters from Iceland* (1937) is a playful and brilliant book. MacNeice's final contribution is an 'Epilogue' for Auden, borrowing Auden's manner in a friendly gesture, without quite the expertise. It summarises events of the trip: "No great happenings at all", as they "rode and joked and smoked". And it closes the book in seriousness, with a knocking at the door.

Denis Devlin's first book was published in the year of *Letters from Iceland,* in his late twenties. *Intercessions* is full of powerful promise and acts of will; poetry of "a probity" (as Samuel Beckett described it) "depending on a minimum of rational interference...". In 'Death and Her Beasts, Ignoble Beasts' it is the turn of vultures, after a time of noble beasts. An amount of partly managed—sometimes coded—matter settles on this simple image. Devlin's generation is emerging out of a stupor, after the generation of the Civil War. (An Irish disaster: titanic, with its "emerald bergs of doom".) For parts of the poem the material is out of control, the poetry struggling to escape. In another decade, in *Lough Derg and Other Poems* (1946), Devlin's poetry had succeeded.

Beagles, Horses, Bikes, Thighs, Boats, Grass, Bluebells, Rickshaws, Stockings (1940—1949)

Ciaran Carson

I was born in 1948, so my personal memories of that decade are necessarily minimal. But some of its atmosphere leaked through to the early 50s, for I remember books of ration coupons, the smell of gas-masks which survived the War, and the open expanses of the Belfast blitz sites. Of course the Irish Free State was not in the War at all, preferring to call it the Emergency. But I can recognise this dimly-lit period, in which petrol was dispensed by the naggin, and bicycles were worth their weight in gold: in the back streets of 1950s Belfast, the passage of a motor car was an event.

Distances, according to many Southern observers, became appreciably longer, and it was realised that Ireland was a bigger place than it had been for many years. Furthermore, the country was clean, uncluttered and unhurried. The goodness of simple things was emphasized rather than diminished by the absence of superfluous luxuries. The population was exhorted by the Department of Agriculture to grow potatoes wherever possible; and the shortage of British coal encouraged the development of the peat bogs. There was, in any case, a lively black market in nylon stockings and tobacco products, as well as a legitimate supply of top coats, as advertised by Siberrys, Civil and Military Tailors, in

The Bell of November 1940: "Over 400 are awaiting your inspection, and they are a handsome range of reliable Coats. The prices are very moderate, being from 5 guineas upwards"; though clients were cautioned that "owing to the war it is most advisable to buy early this season". No such restriction applied to PYE radios, also widely advertised in *The Bell* throughout the Emergency: these were distinguished from "the mass-produced receivers" by their being "calibrated and tuned in Ireland to suit Irish conditions"; they were, in fact, "sound as a Bell".

In many ways the Ireland of the 1940s seemed to resemble a de Valeran ideal; *The Bell,* founded by Sean O'Faolain at the beginning of the decade, dedicated itself to undermining nationalistic pieties. It also made a point of publishing writers from Northern Ireland, such as John Hewitt, Colin Middleton, Roy McFadden, Michael McLaverty, and W.R. Rodgers. Louis MacNeice was poetry editor for a brief spell. "MacNeice, born in Belfast, of Irish family, is almost wholly Irish in origin; but almost wholly English in his work. In him the tradition of voluntary transplantation has its latest notable example. He has written poems with Irish subjects and some Irish feeling; but all told he is an English poet so far", wrote Robert Farren in *The Course of Irish Verse,* published by Sheed & Ward in 1948. Farren—or Roibeárd Ó Faracháin, as he sometimes styled himself—was a poet of some reputation, but was handicapped, according to Austin Clarke, by having his work published by "a propagandist religious firm, and, to find his work, we must, as often as not, brave the plaster statues and sensational tracts of repositories". Ó Faracháin would hardly have approved of MacNeice's comment on the Free State's separatist stance, 'Neutrality', written in September 1942:

> But then look eastward from your heart, there bulks
> A continent, close, dark, as archetypal sin,
> While to the west off your own shores the mackerel
> Are fat—on the flesh of your kin.

Irishness was an issue. As articulated by Farren:

> "There have been among younger poets the customary rebellions. Some were so much in revolt against their elders, and so fetched by the louder music of English and American literary concert-halls, that they walked right out of their own doors trying to be at home across the street. They seemed to want to write like the Eliots and the Audens. It would not be true to claim that they all came back to their own house; but the signs are strong that they are one by one returning; and if one or two are loitering on the pathway, the family voices are not failing to reach their ears.
>
> In this connexion the poets to the North-East are especially interesting. Partition has by now become spiritual in some of those who live in the Six Counties; and a poet like John Hewitt is strongly aware of his position. But all that we mean by Ireland is holding them from absorption into English poetry; and if the grip can be seen in Hewitt it has all but suceeded entirely with Rodgers. A markedly Irish temperament and a love of the Irish country keep him with the covey. His recent removal to London may have its effect, but we shall see.
>
> In the Twenty-six counties of course the Irish ethos works more vigorously. Self-government and all that produced and flows from it, help our literary separatism, which we believe in not because it is separatism but because it is the habit of all healthy nations. Did Goethe, Villon, Dante, Ibsen, Johnson, Calderon lose or gain as writers through their being wholly German, French, Italian, English, Norwegian, or Spanish, each his own?"

W.R. ("Bertie") Rodgers, like most Irish poets at the time, North or South, was published in England. Secker & Warburg's first printing of his first book, *Awake! And Other Poems,* was destroyed by the blitz on Plymouth in 1940; a second printing was brought out in 1941. From 1934 to 1946, when he went to the BBC in London at the invitation of Louis MacNeice, Rodgers was the minister of Cloveneden Church, Loughgall, Co. Armagh, in which parish the Orange Order had been founded. Fond of whiskey and verbal acrobatics, he became known to his congregation as "the

Catholic Presbyterian". Dan Davin, in an introductory memoir to Rodgers' *Collected Poems,* tells of "how the pulpit in Loughgall was so high that, on those Sundays when Saturday had been the night before, Bertie—as even that staid parish knew its pastor—could stoop in a pause of his preaching, at some cautiously contrived colon, and retch gently, invisible to his devout and Sunday-sombre flock". Davin supposed him to be "the Presbyterian equivalent of a 'spoiled priest'".

With drink taken, Rodgers would employ "Scheherezade's technique of the unended anecdote, like unclosed parentheses, so you could never cut him off"; though sometimes individual pieces in the monologue were short and to the point. To illustrate the love-hate between North and South he could recall the man challenged at the Border. "Friend or foe?" No reply and your man comes on, boots loud in the dark. "Friend or foe? Answer or I fire." "Foe." "Pass, foe."

I cannot fully gauge the impact that Rodgers' first book made on the poetry-reading public at the time; but today, some of the writing is still astonishingly fresh: "Suddenly all the fountains in the park/ Opened smoothly their umbrellas of water" ('The Fountain'); "And I was left here in the darkened house/ Listening for the fat click of the softly-shut door" ('The Interned Refugee').

'Beagles' is a parable, some say of the relationship with his wife, Marie Harden Waddell, who became the village doctor in Loughgall, where she grew mentally unstable and developed an addiction to morphine. But the controlled headlong rhythms owe much to the many songs, still to be found in the County Armagh, which celebrate and empathize with the hunted hare. "Nothing pleases me so much in writing," said Rodgers, "as to be able to sit on both sides of the sense, and if there were six sides I would sit on them all."

Fitting words for a diplomat, perhaps, if not a minister of religion. Much of Valentin Iremonger's life was spent as a diplomat: he was Irish ambassador to Sweden, Norway, Finland, Luxembourg, and Portugal; and the poem by which he is represented here reminds me of a childhood anecdote of another poet and diplomat, Pablo Neruda:

> "… one day while hunting behind my house for the tiny objects and miniscule beings of my worlds, I discovered a hole in one of the fence boards. I looked through the opening and saw a patch of land just like ours, untended and wild. I drew back a few steps, because I had a vague feeling that something was about to happen. Suddenly a hand came through. It was the small hand of a boy my own age. When I moved closer, the hand was gone and in its place was a little white sheep.
>
> It was a sheep made of wool that had faded. The wheels on which it glided were gone. I had never seen such a lovely sheep. I went into my house and came back with a gift, which I left in the same place: a pine cone, partly open, fragrant and resinous, and very precious to me.
>
> I never saw the boy's hand again. I have never seen a little sheep like that one. I lost it in a fire. And even today, when I go past a toy shop, I look in the window furtively. But it's no use. A sheep like that one was never made again."

In such exchanges of gifts are the beginnings of diplomacy. Iremonger's poem about the toy horse was originally published in *The Bell* of September 1942 as 'Poem', which might be a better title than 'The Toy Horse'. Patrick Kavanagh in his survey, 'Poetry in Ireland Today', also in *The Bell*, of April 1948, quoted from it appreciatively, for, though it "gave promise of talent which time has not fulfilled", it had "a charming innocence of originality", and was one of the few bits of contemporary writing that satisfied his criteria:

> "Sean Ó Faolain suggested, and sever other superficial critics supported him, that I was only interested in flat reality; that I had dung in my mouth, that I only understood the small farm. For everything outside that I had no understanding or love.
>
> Nothing could be further from the truth. What I seek and love when I find is the whiskey of the imagination, not the bread and butter of 'reality'. This is the thing I seek in writing and this is the thing I most dreadfully miss in the verse

that is being written in this country these days. The poems being written are like perfectly laid-out corpses on a slab. They are perfectly shaped and perfectly dead."

Kavanagh did not call it "Irish Poetry", but "Poetry in Ireland". For Kavanagh, poetry was universal: "We must record love's mystery without claptrap,/ Snatch out of time the passionate transitory." Kavanagh shared with Frank O'Connor the distinction of coming to the attention of the Free State Censorship Board: Kavanagh for 'The Great Hunger', O'Connor for his translation of Brian Merriman's 18th century classic, 'Cúirt an Mhéan-Oíche', published in 1945 as 'The Midnight Court'. Both works were passionate critiques of the de Valeran State—'The Great Hunger' directly, 'The Midnight Court' by implication, and perhaps all the more of an insult to the authorities because they could not deny that it was Irish.

In his study of the short story, *The Lonely Voice,* O'Connor makes the point that "there is in the short story at its most characteristic something we do not often find in the novel—an intense awareness of human loneliness." The short story is perhaps not that far removed from poetry: Kavanagh voices that loneliness in his best work; so, in a very different way, does Louis MacNeice. 'The Cyclist' (dated September, 1946) has been a favourite poem of mine since I first read it some time in the late 60s; in fact, one of my first published poems was an unconscious pastiche of it (I am embarrassed to recall that it was called 'Cyclist: Danger, gradient 1 in 6'). It seemed to me that MacNeice's linguistic embodiment of sensual joy and fear was an accurate record of experience; now, the philosophical overtones seem a shade heavy.

Denis Devlin—another diplomat—was not averse to philosophy, and some of the poems in which he built a reputation suffer from it. 'Memo from a Millionaire' (from *Lough Derg and Other Poems,* 1946) can be read as a Jansenist parable, but it is also a pleasurable skit, and some of the rhymes are great fun, with their echoes of Browning, Swift and Byron; even, perhaps, of 'The Midnight Court'. There are also European influences, but paradoxically, 'Memo from a Millionaire' seems to me a very Irish poem, if being Irish means to play about with a language that is not wholly yours: it has elements of the hedge-school about it.

Donagh MacDonagh's 'The Hungry Grass' (1947) is, of course, indubitably Irish, if we overlook the sometimes Audenesque cadences. He was the son of the Thomas MacDonagh who was a signatory of the Proclamation of the Irish Republic, and he rose to become a District Justice, a position which no doubt afforded him convenient opportunities to indulge his interest in folklore. 'The Hungry Grass' is a poem which I half-expected to find in Walton's *Treasury of Irish Songs and Ballads.* I have just checked, and it is not there, but it has that folky Victorian melodramatic recitative air about it: no bad thing, for if poetry aspires to be memorable, this is a memorable poem. It also corresponds to O'Connor's "lonely voice", and O'Connor's quotation from Gogol, "from that day forth everything was as it were changed, and appeared in a different light to him."

A different light pervades Kavanagh's 'Bluebells for Love'. All Kavanagh's poetry is bathed in light: here, it is a flicker, something glimpsed from the corner of the eye, a shock of *déjà vu.* It is about time passing as it is remembered or seen "glance by glance" through a lover's eyes. I much prefer this Kavanagh to the tub-thumper of 'The Great Hunger', which still contains beautiful details, like the description of the card players, like a Breughel lit by Caravaggio. Later, Kavanagh claimed to disown 'The Great Hunger':

> "In 1942 I wrote *The Great Hunger.* Shortly after it was published a couple of hefty lads came to my lonely shieling on Pembroke Road. One of them had a copy of the poem behind his back. He broght it to the front and he asked me, 'Did you write that?' He was a policeman. It may seem shocking to the devotee of liberalism if I say that the police were right. For a poet in his true detachment is impervious to policeman. There is something wrong with a work of art, some kinetic vulgarity in it when it is visible to policemen."

John Hewitt's encounters with the guardians of faith and morals were less spectacular; but he believed that he had been passed over for promotion by the trustees of the Belfast Museum and Art Gallery, where he worked for many years, because of his avowed socialist sympathies. Piqued by this alleged bias, he went to Coventry, where he became Director of the Herbert Art Gallery. 'From a Museum Man's Album', first published in *The Bell* of March 1948, shows him escaping his assiduous iambics for a comparatively anecdotal treatment.

Hewitt sometimes pondered his relationship with what he called "the Irishry", and his poem 'Gloss, on the Difficulties of Translation', features the famous 9th century Irish poem about the blackbird of Belfast Lough, which had fascinated him for some forty years. Seán Ó Ríordáin's 'Malairt' has not engrossed me that long, but I have been trying to translate it for about half of my life. The title itself is untranslatable. Dinneen gives the word a full column in his *Irish-English Dictionary*. Among other things, it is glossed as "a change, alteration (as in a text), exchange, swop, barter, dealing, traffic, recompense; difference, variety, opposite". It can, I think, mean translation, or metamorphosis. It is about one's relationship to language; Irish, to Ó Ríordáin, was *"an teanga seo leath-liom"* (this language half-mine). I published a version of 'Malairt' in my collection *First Language*. The version here is yet another.

Lucky's speech, monologue, or tirade in *Waiting for Godot* is language on the verge of breakdown; so it behaves like poetry. It reminds me of nothing so much as the speech of a character in a Belfast pub, The Spanish Rooms (long since demolished), known colloquially as "The Scrumpy Rooms" for the immense quantities of cheap cider it dispensed. Louie's monologues were similarly larded with cliché and impressive philosophical references. His words shone like a beacon in mid-60s, pre-Troubles Belfast, where the monochromatic gloom of the 40s still seemed to throw its shadow. And I was encouraged to quote Lucky's tirade as poetry because, in the course of researching this essay, I learned that Beckett began writing *Godot* on the 9th of October, 1948, my birthday.

Scylla and Charybdis (1950—1959)

JOHN MONTAGUE

M ake no mistake about it, when I was starting out, *all* the senior Irish poets (except MacNeice, because of Faber) were neglected. Clarke might intone on "Radio Iran" (Kavanagh's acid quip), or Kavanagh himself groan like an angry foghorn through Grafton Street, but they were not in print. Not only were they not in print, but they were fighting among themselves, like Kilkenny cats. And yet, perhaps partly because of that strife, at the end of the decade Irish poetry was again in full sail, for the first time since the death of Yeats.

But back to the beginning of my story. In 1950, *Anno Santo*, the Holy Year, I was twenty-one, with my heart set on going to Rome by way of Paris, Salzburg, Vienna and Venice. Matteradam I had very little money; I was on my way. Brendan Behan had given me a few addresses for Paris, but beyond that I was on my own, which was the way I wanted it. For Ireland, and its capital, Dublin, seemed to me a fen of stagnant waters (or writers) for someone like myself who wished to write poetry and/or prose. So I shook the rust of Ireland off my feet, and hied away for a few crucial months to explore broken post-war Europe, and discover my own proper loneliness. There is a sequence by my friend Michael Hamburger, which shows that my experience was part of a generation, a sequence called 'Notes of a European tramp'.

Meanwhile, back in Dublin, the poetry wars were hotting up.

Decades are untidy things, and the first salvo had really been fired by Kavanagh, in an extraordinary essay on Yeats's pal, F. R. Higgins, which bewildered me when I read it, during a lecture in the old UCD Physics Theatre. Called 'The Gallivanting Poet' (*Irish Writing 3*) it seemed to argue that Higgins was fake, because he was a Protestant pretending to be a Celtic Catholic, a new kind of sectarianism which threw me off balance because, although I was from Ulster, I had never expected to encounter it in literary criticism. A mid-century chiliasm throbbed behind the words: "Now is the time for silent prayer and long fasting. Literature as we have known it has come to the end of its tether." It was followed by a similar attack in *The Bell* on Frank O'Connor, 'Coloured Balloons', challenging his authenticity as a recorder of Irish life.

Shortly after I returned from my mini *wanderjahre*, a new magazine, *Envoy*, began, with Kavanagh (whom Val Iremonger, its poetry editor, called Kafka) blasting and bombadiering in its 'Diary'. Walking along Grafton Street in the company of another young poet, I saw a large shambling man, hat shoved on his head, plunging down the other side of the street. "That's Patrick Kavanagh," announced my companion, "I *hate* that man!". Clearly, no one could be indifferent to this uncompromising figure, but unlike my fellow poet I felt drawn to him.

Kavanagh was striving towards a definition of the authentic in Irish life, through an analysis of its opposite, something called 'buck lepping', a strident form of Irishness that played to the gallery. *Envoy* collapsed, and was followed by *Kavanagh's Weekly*. I recall a strange meeting with Patrick and his brother in Bewley's that summer, both showing the big toe in outsize sandals. "You're a very nervous young man," flapped Kavanagh, "but I wouldn't be surprised if you had some merit." We discussed a possible contribution, but he was already wearying of the blunderbuss and bludgeon. "Satire is a double-edged sword, it cuts the hand that wields it." His brother Peter was silent, dismissive of this almost unpublished young idealist.

Kavanagh was not writing poetry at the time: he was clearing the decks, seemingly in order to walk the plank. But when his admirer and friend, Anthony Cronin, became assistant editor of *The Bell,* he and Peadar O'Donnell began to coax poems out of Kavanagh with hard cash, lovely poems like 'Prelude' which expressed the self-criticism I had sensed, "Give us another poem, he said/ Or they will think your muse is dead;/ Another middle-aged departure/ Of Apollo from the trade of archer."

Kavanagh's campaign routed the champions of the Irish or neo-Gaelic mode. Robert Farren, whose work Kavanagh described in his *Envoy Diary* as "frivolity laid on with a navvy shovel", fell silent, although his *First Exile* (1944), a long poem on Colmcille, had been a big success, and his *Course* (now dubbed "Curse") *of Irish Verse* was a textbook for advocates of the Irish mode. Austin Clarke was also under fire. His conservative Cultural Relations pamphlet, *Poetry in Modern Ireland* (1951), which scanted Kavanagh and elevated F.R. Higgins and Farren, aroused great ire among the McDaids' troops. For the poetic wars had spread to the pubs, where Irish writers had moved after the demise of the dignified salons of the Literary Revival. During the isolation of the War years, euphemistically called "the Emergency", most writers congregated in the lofty-ceilinged Palace Bar: there is a famous picture of the "standing army" of Irish writers. As the ideological divide grew, the older writers moved to The Pearl, across from *The Irish Times,* while the young consorted with Kavanagh in the more *farouche* McDaids. Or so it seemed, but human affairs are always more complicated. John Jordan exchanged affectionate obscenities with Kavanagh, Cronin discussed racing form, Myles scowled, Hutchinson praised yet another book, Behan trotted through, and I even dared to enter myself. It was a scene that would be well described by Iremonger in the *Leader* profile of Kavanagh, which led to Kavanagh's unwise libel action.

What was the root of these wars? It was an Irish version of the perennial dispute between the Ancient and the Modern, involving one step forward and one step back. In the *Faber Book of Contemporary Irish Verse* (1949), Valentine Iremonger and Robert Greacen declared themselves for a multiplicity of styles. Iremonger, a lean Dublin civil servant with a slight cast in one eye, had been the apostle of the Modern in Ireland, with articles in *The Bell* on all the modern British poets. But when someone like MacNeice did come through, with his side-kick W.R. Rodgers, it was usually to record BBC radio programmes on the past, on the great dead figures of the Literary Revival. They were a dangerously seductive pair to meet, the lean intelligent face of MacNeice, Rodgers' deceptively gentle sibilance, as they cruised all day through Dublin, from the Tower bar (the Radio Éireann pub in Henry Street) to the Pearl; I even once saw MacNeice slumped in McDaids, although that was much later. But the real centre of the maelstrom was the outsize personality of Patrick Kavanagh.

In 1953, I took off again, this time to America. Ireland seemed to be the Slough of Despond, with Kavanagh growing more grumpy, and *The Bell* sounding dimmer for a second time: Cronin's editorials of the period groaned like a foghorn in thick mist, as if the island was drowning. This coming and going was part of the decade, as we sought to come to terms with our sour little country. Hutchinson and Jordan seemed to find a refuge in Barcelona, and Cronin was soon to leave, too, for a longer time in southern Spain.

When I came back three years later, things had begun to get better, mainly because of Liam Miller and his Dolmen Press, the first poetry press in Ireland since the Cuala, and with an equally high standard of design. They had produced Tom Kinsella's first frail book, *Poems* (1956), and would foster his *Another September* (1958), the first Irish book to be a Choice of the Poetry Book Society. And Clarke was being reluctantly reborn, perhaps in response to all the taunts, the hostile atmosphere. *Ancient Lights* (1955) gathered together older favourites like 'The Blackbird of Derrycairn', from his play *The Crow Flies,* but also introspective, angry poems like 'Ancient Lights', to be followed in two years by *Too Great a Vine,* which contains my favourite Clarke longer poem, 'The Loss of Strength', compressing our early religious history with glittering technique:

Too great a vine, they say, can sour
The best of clay. No pair of sinners
But learned saints had overpowered
Our country, Malachi the Thin
And Bernard of Clairvaux. Prodigious
In zeal, these cooled and burned our porridge.
(Later came breakspear, strong bow backing)
The arch sprang wide for their Cistercians.
O bread was wersh and well was brack.
War rattled at us in hammered shirts:
An Englishman had been the Pontiff.
They marched to Mellifont.

Although most of my day was taken up with my job at Bord
Fáilte (the only one I could find), I was beginning to assemble my
own slim first volume, *Forms of Exile* (1958). Between the Scylla of
craftsman Clarke and the Charybdis of an angry Kavanagh, I had
lived out my Irish poetic Fifties, and now things were looking up.
I recall a series of readings in the Eblana Theatre, perhaps the first
public performances by poets for a long time; Kavanagh probably
never gave a poetry reading in his life, being born long before what
Cronin exasperatedly calls 'the great Poetry Boom'. People assumed
the usual masks of deference to conceal their boredom and unease,
but when Kinsella read 'Baggot Street Deserta', even the
Chairman, Paddy Browne of Galway, woke up: "It's great to hear
such intelligent poetry again."

I read with Máire Mhac an tSaoi, part, with Seán Ó Ríordáin
and Máirtín Ó Direáin, of the New Wave of Irish poetry in Irish,
which had come alive again during the War years, when Ireland
drew back into herself. And with Patrick Galvin, whose 'My Little
Red Knife' sent shudders through the more respectable sections of
the audience: Miss O'Flaherty of Parsons Bookshop shook her
metaphorical rosary at him when he read lines like "I kissed and
kissed a thousand lies/ And opened wide her golden thighs/ To
please my little red knife". Galvin had been working in England,
but he and Ewart Milne were to return, to swell the new poetry
scene. There were still few women, and they tended to be "lady

poets". I knew that delicate pianist, Rhoda Coghill, whose 'Bright Hillside' I admired. Brendan Behan's future mother-in-law, Blanaid Salkeld, published *Experiment in Error* (1958), at the age of seventy-five. And there was Freda Laughton and Temple Lane, mild pioneers of a story still to come. Nearly ten years after the Faber anthology, the *Oxford Book of Irish Verse,* edited by Donagh MacDonagh and Lennox Robinson, tried to set the clock back, but the 60s had already begun.

A Boat on the River (1960—1969)

MICHAEL LONGLEY

For me the 60s began quietly in Dublin and ended tumultuously in Belfast. When the decade began I was half way through my career as a lapsed Classicist at Trinity College. My undergraduate friends and acquaintances included the poets Derek Mahon, Rudi Holzapfel, Brendan Kennelly and, some time later, Eavan Boland. On campus Holzapfel was the most talked-about poet, followed closely by Kennelly with whom he co-published a couple of early (premature) collections. The height of my own ambition in 1960 was to have poems accepted by the college literary magazine *Icarus*. There were no workshops or writers' groups in those days, and very few poetry readings. "Creative Writing" as an academic activity was not on the menu at Trinity. Rather, we hoped that we were free spirits rebelling against scholarly restriction. But a few professors—in my case the great Homeric scholar W.B. Stanford, himself once an aspiring poet—did keep an eye on our lyrical strivings. And there was one life-enhancing, larger-than-life English lecturer who inspired us all, Alec Reid. We considered it an honour to traipse beside his rotund figure as, nearly blind, he trundled to a favourite pub enthusing about Louis MacNeice or Edward Thomas. The *genius loci,* the true patron of *Icarus,* he challenged us to fly and picked up the fallen feathers.

Extraordinarily, there was next to no literary interchange between TCD and UCD (let alone Cork where Eiléan Ní Chuilleanáin was a student). If we Trinity poets were learning from each other, how much more skilled and versed we might have become had we jousted with the likes of Michael Hartnett, Eamon Grennan and, later, Paul Durcan who were inhabiting a parallel universe in Earlsfort Terrace. We did get a whiff of UCD at its best when, in 1962, John Jordan revived *Poetry Ireland*. Submissions were returned thoughtfully annotated, sometimes at length. It was then a rigorously skinny magazine and acceptance mattered a lot. Jordan took our apprentice pieces seriously. The same was true of Terence de Vere White who found space on the single literary page of the Saturday *Irish Times* for the first paid appearances of most of my generation, brief lyrics in black boxes. The apogee of this generous patronage came some years later when David Marcus founded *New Irish Writing*. Every Saturday a whole page of the *Irish Press* was devoted to prose and poetry hot off the typewriter. It seemed important that imaginative writing was being published in a newspaper rather than in the *cordon sanitaire* of a literary magazine. Marcus's acute, expansive editorship brought together young writers from all over Ireland and educated them about each other. This was sorely needed after the doldrums of the introspective 50s and the death of such a brilliant star as the literary and cultural monthly, *The Bell*, with its deliberate policy of including writers from Northern Ireland.

The first contemporary Irish collection I got to know was a Belfast friend's copy of John Montague's *Forms of Exile*, which I brought with me to Trinity. The publication of a slim volume was then a rare and significant occasion. We collected and exchanged the early books of Montague, Thomas Kinsella, Richard Murphy, Pearse Hutchinson, most of them beautifully produced by Liam Miller of the Dolmen Press, mastermind and virtuoso printer. His small firm put Irish publishing on the world map, and his very presence was an inspiration. Many of us dreamed of being taken on by Dolmen. Even so, England and a larger readership beckoned. Murphy went to Faber with *Sailing to an Island* which generated in the *Irish Times* a controversy about metrics. Montague, whose *Poisoned Lands* had been published by the London firm of MacGibbon & Kee, helped to bring about the appearance under that imprint of two important volumes of *Collected Poems,* John Hewitt's and Patrick Kavanagh's. Timothy O'Keefe, the enlightened crusader for Irish poetry at MacGibbon & Kee, wrote in the *Listener* that the cultural worth of a publishing house could be judged by the strength of its poetry list. Are we living in the Dark Ages today? In the 60s a small number of remarkable editorial talents helped to generate enlightenment and a sense of literary community.

By 1964 I had moved back to Belfast where Philip Hobsbaum, an English lecturer at Queen's University, invited me to join his literary powerhouse, The Group. This met regularly for vigorous critical discussion of new writing, often in an atmosphere of nervy exhilaration. Hobsbaum encouraged us to believe that good work could come out of a locale as unpromising as Belfast ("a cultural Sahara" according to some). In the *Spectator* he forecast the city's cultural consequence. I met Seamus Heaney at The Group, but, contrary to the mythology, Derek Mahon attended only once or twice. And, at the time of my involvement, James Simmons was teaching in Nigeria, Stewart Parker in the States. Heaney was my first Northern Irish Catholic friend. With segregated schooling and the Ban forbidding Catholics to attend Trinity, an invisible apartheid had been skillfully concocted. Until my friendship with him, I had barely registered the cultural damage. I introduced Heaney to Mahon and Heaney introduced me to Simmons. We were intensely aware of each other's work, but there were no agendas or manifestos. The only programme was an invigorating rush for recognition and publication. (Our two main Irish outlets were the recrudescent *Dublin Magazine* and *Phoenix* which Harry Chambers had brought from Liverpool to Belfast. We also submitted poems to British journals.) Looking back to Rimbaud some of us in our mid-twenties were feeling like slow starters. Between 1966 and 1969 we all brought out our first collections. Simmons also founded the now famous *Honest Ulsterman* in 1968. It was far too rumbustious ever to be considered a house magazine. Its lack of cosiness reflected our friendships.

Eavan Boland paid a few whirlwind visits to Belfast with news of what was happening in Dublin. Over the next few years certain developments indicated that the map of poetry would now have to be redrawn to include Belfast. A series of pamphlets by, among others, Heaney, Mahon, Simmons and Seamus Deane was published under the aegis of the new Belfast Festival. In 1968 the Arts Council of Northern Ireland promoted *Room to Rhyme,* a poetry reading tour of the province which featured Heaney, myself and the folk singer David Hammond. (A similar tour was undertaken by Montague and Hewitt in 1970. Roy Foster has called *The Planter and the Gael* "a landmark affirmation of creative cultural diversity". Retrospectively, a similar claim could be made for *Room to Rhyme.*) In his spectacularly successful first and second collections, *Death of a Naturalist* and *Door into the Dark,* Heaney created from the Derry countryside and the smallholdings around Bellaghy his "soul-landscape", to borrow Beckett's coinage, and brought to light a "hidden Ulster". Mahon did something similar for the city of Belfast in several of the dazzling lyrics which make *Night Crossing* one of the most prodigious debuts in the history of poetry. In his first two collections Simmons released into the mainstream of Irish verse the energies of the popular song. The publication of John Hewitt's *Collected Poems* and his lovely, welcoming review of *Death of a Naturalist* in the *Belfast Telegraph* reminded us of an absent friend. The news that he had bought a house in Stockman's Lane and would be returning with his wife to live in Belfast after a fifteen year exile felt like a blessing.

What we inadequately call "the Troubles" created a further kind of mutual awareness among poets from the North. No one wanted to hitch a ride on yesterday's headlines; to write, if I may misquote John Hume, the poetry of the latest atrocity. The notion that poetry might provide solace for the grief of others also repelled us. Ten years after the first explosions I wrote about what I was trying to do in my fourth collection *The Echo Gate* and, I dare to hope, in my earlier work: "Though the poet's first duty must be to his imagination, he has other obligations—and not just as a citizen. He would be inhuman if he did not respond to tragic events in his own community, and a poor artist if he did not seek to endorse that response imaginatively. But if his imagination fails him, the result will be a dangerous impertinence. In the context of political violence the deployment of words at their most precise and most suggestive remains one of the few antidotes to death-dealing dishonesty." As I said in the opening sentence of this essay, for me the 60s ended tumultuously in Belfast. But the turmoil has racked the whole island. Some of the noblest responses to the tragedy have come from southern poets, most notably Paul Durcan whose eloquence is born of anguish.

I sometimes wonder what MacNeice and Kavanagh would make of it all, both of them dying before their time and before the outbreak of the Troubles, MacNeice in 1963 (just days before the publication of *The Burning Perch* in which the lyric poem reaches a fearful new frontier), Kavanagh in 1967. He had declared that his "purpose in life was to have no purpose"; that his ambition was "to play a true note on a dead slack string". Thirty years of atrocities are refracted proleptically and most terribly in his seminal sonnet 'Epic' ("I have lived in important places, times / When great events were decided …"). The closing line of MacNeice's 'Charon' faces into nightmare on behalf of the unremembered and the disapppeared: "If you want to die you will have to pay for it." He nearly called his last book *Funeral Games,* a far more telling title than *The Burning Perch.* His friend and BBC colleague, the Ulster poet W.R. Rodgers, was the honoured guest when Mahon gave a paper on MacNeice to Trinity's Philosophical Society. Happily on the fringe of that occasion, I spoke to the paper, but about a year later failed to rise to the challenge when Mahon proposed that we introduce ourselves to MacNeice who was provoking the regulars up the road in McDaid's. I now rue my reluctance. I did, however, spend a sunny spring afternoon in that pub with Kavanagh who, having refused to give the promised interview for a college magazine, bought the penniless student pints and chasers over several rollicking hours. He was wonderful, preternaturally sensitive beneath the boorish exterior, foul mouthed and beatific. When I sat next to Austin Clarke at the Kennellys' wedding reception, all he said to me was: "Would you pass the salt, please."

Studying our elders with a real sense of involvement, we were impressed by Clarke's burden of "golden chains" but anxious that he might collapse under their weight; we were relieved that after the middle-aged doldrums of *Autumn Sequel* and *Ten Burnt Offerings* MacNeice's sails were billowing again; we felt confused by the mixture of the casual and the exquisite in Kavanagh's *Come Dance with Kitty Stobling*. We read aloud to each other Montague's 'The Trout' and 'All Legendary Obstacles'. We had by heart Kinsella's lilting lines, "Soft, to your places, animals, / Your legendary duty calls." We theorised about the syllabic patterning of Murphy's 'Sailing to an Island' and 'The Cleggan Disaster'. Anthologies such as Donald Hall's *Contemporary American Poetry, The New Poetry* edited by A. Alvarez and Michael Roberts' *The Faber Book of Modern Verse* were a further education and primed us for Larkin and Hughes, Lowell and Wilbur. We collected for a few shillings each that inspired paperback series, the *Penguin Modern European Poets:* Akhmatova, Rilke, Enzensberger, Montale. We were appraising our roots and at the same time scanning the horizon.

One journey has become symbolic in my memory. In the summer of 1965 Derek Mahon, my wife and I hitch-hiked around Connemara and County Clare. We sailed to Inishmore and were drenched in sunshowers; and we visited Jack Sweeney's Irish retreat in Corofin (Terence de Vere White had told him about us). The founder of the celebrated Poetry Room at Harvard, Sweeney had recorded many of the great modern poets long before the value of sound archive was appreciated. In my Trinity rooms Mahon and I had played again and again a compilation which included the sing-song E.E. Cummings, Robert Frost, William Carlos Williams who sounded like a corncrake, and our favourite, the mango-rich tones of Wallace Stevens reciting 'The Idea of Order at Key West'. We were delighted to learn that "Fat Wal" as we called him (an irreverent allusion to the portliness both of his figure and his *Collected Poems*) had written his poem 'The Irish Cliffs of Moher' after receiving a picture postcard from his friends Jack and Máire Sweeney. So much came together at that lunch in Corofin. We were joined by the house-guest Richard Eberhardt whose voice we had often listened to reading his best poem 'The Groundhog' on the same record. Sweeney continued to send us folded airletters packed with wise disinterested comments on our early efforts. Considering how little we had published, it was an extraordinary endorsement when he arranged for some of us to be recorded in Dublin for the Harvard Poetry Room. The Burren and the Aran Islands still evoke for me those first embarkations. Perhaps poets should always remain newcomers.

As I think back to the friendships of the 60s, I find myself believing again in a sodality of the imagination. Or, as Eugenio Montale puts it: "Only the isolated communicate. The others—the men of mass communication—repeat, echo, vulgarise the words of the poets. And although these are not words of faith today, they might well become so in the future." In his beautiful poem 'The Friendship of Young Poets' Douglas Dunn regrets that "My youth was as private/ As the bank at midnight", and conjures up an ideal scene:

> There is a boat on the river now, and
> Two young men, one rowing, one reading aloud.
> Their shirt sleeves fill with wind, and from the oars
> Drop scales of perfect river like melting glass.

Meaning Business (1970—1979)

Seamus Heaney

Internment, Bloody Sunday, Sunningdale, Ewart-Biggs: the 70s involve more than nostalgia for flares and sideburns. And more than the politics and atrocities of the North: this was the decade when Mary Robinson and Nell McCafferty made their mark in the Republic, when the womens movement organized and gathered force, when the fact that "wife who smashes television gets jail" became a matter of common concern. It was also a decade when Irish poets faced with new urgency all the old problems of how to be true to their art while living with their obligations and exacerbations as members of a society in crisis.

For poetry, it was a period of extraordinary richness. In the first three years there appeared Seán Ó Ríordáin's *Línte Liombó,* John Montague's *The Rough Field,* Thomas Kinsella's *New Poems,* Pearse Hutchinson's *Watching the Morning Grow,* Derek Mahon's *Lives,* Michael Longley's *An Exploded View,* James Simmons's *Energy to Burn,* Eiléan Ní Chuilleanáin's *Acts and Monuments,* and Paul Muldoon's *New Weather.* Anthony Cronin returned to the scene with a *Collected Poems* in 1972 and Padraic Fallon's *Collected,* a restitution and a revelation, came out in 1974. The middle of the decade saw the publication of the first full collection by Paul Durcan (*O Westport in the Light of Asia Minor*) and Ciaran Carson (*The New Estate*). New turns occurred in the work of Eavan Boland

and Michael Hartnett, in *The War Horse* and *A Farewell to English* respectively, both of which appeared in 1975. Richard Murphy's work refreshed itself by relocating in *High Island* (a book which also contained an imaginative bilocation in the Ceylon of his childhood) and John Hewitt continued to reap the rewards of return to his native Belfast in the three volumes published in 1974, 1976 and 1978. Meanwhile, Tom Paulin's voice was first heard in *A State of Justice* (1977) while Brendan Kennelly's *Love Cry* (1972) and *The Voices* (1973) were the first of five collections he would issue over the course of the decade. In Cork, in 1978, Seán Ó Tuama published *Saol Fó Thoinn* and was simultaneously nourishing a group of new poets who would change the course of poetry in the Irish language during the 80s and 90s. And in Belfast, as the decade ended, Medbh McGuckian began to write the unexpected and beguiling lyrics that would complicate the picture of "Northern Poetry" as something produced as if on demand by the "famous revolution".

With so much available, it follows that many poems of the 70s which would figure in a more inclusive personal anthology are not to be found here. John Hewitt's 'The King's Horses,' for example; from the moment I read it, I regarded it as one of his strangest and truest lyrics, a poem about his own poetic calling, based on those "intuitions, intimations, imaginative realizations, epiphanies" which, as he said in his 1972 essay, 'No Rootless Colonist', "may not be the worst way to face life and its future in our bitter, hate-riven island." Another favourite, not included, that came home to me on first encounter and has stayed with me ever since is Padraic Fallon's 'Gurteen', a poem which is at once a manifestation of the truth of Patrick Kavanagh's famous statement in 'Epic' that "Gods make their own importance", and a revision of it, "the epic, if any, going on too long". Nor was I able to fit in the high lament of Richard Murphy's 'Seals at High Island', a poem where Murphy returned with great confidence to a kind of large formal utterance he had mastered in the 60s, discovering a personal fable in an elemental scenario.

When it came to picking the final ten, I gave the space to representatives of younger generations, those coming into their full creative power as the decade began and those who were just beginning to strike their true note. In 1972, for example, Thomas Kinsella's *Notes from the Land of the Dead* appeared in a limited edition, and from that moment an indeflectible exploration of the self and its agons was under way in this poet's work. Kinsella served notice of the intent and seriousness of his effort by the complete certitude in the early poems of the series ("Something that had— clenched in its cave — / not been now was: an egg of being") and emphasized his commitment by issuing it in separate volumes from his own Peppercanister Press. The fact that the first poem to appear from the press was his fierce, head-on assault on the British cover-up of what actually happened on Bloody Sunday only underlined the independence and resolution of what he had undertaken.

Kinsella's poems draw a firm artistic line around themselves, insisting upon themselves as "work"; and yet they manage to do what artistic work always wants to do, they "get at life". The concluding section of 'His Father's Hands', for example, is a description of what to some eyes would look like an ordinary old block of wood stippled with little cobbler's nails, and yet under this poet's gaze it drops into place ("an axis / of light flashing down its length") with all the dream force and arbitrariness of that other great image of the early 70s, the glistening column rearing up out of earth in the opening sequence of Kubrick's *2001: A Space Odyssey*. This ability to combine a fidelity to what is intransigent in the actual and endured with what is luminous when hoarded "in the yolk of one's being, so to speak," gives Kinsella's poem great purchase and is a distinguishing feature of many of those other poems I have chosen to print in this selection.

The poems here, of course, have been chosen as much by "the age" as by myself. No selection of Irish poetry from the 70s could leave out Derek Mahon's 'A Disused Shed in County Wexford'. This poem is now simply part of our culture's dialogue with itself, and that "our" extends well beyond those who live in Ireland to include every individual conscious of the need to live something like an examined life in a dark time. The poem's intellectual *furor* means that it does earnestly hold the belief that "our naive labours have been in vain," and yet, as in all great poetic achievement, there is a residually transcendent trust implicit in the very radiance and consonance and integrity of the poem itself.

A recent commentator on Virgil's *Eclogues* (David Ferry, in his introduction to a new translation) remarks how "the book has sustained and nourished multifarious interpretations and resolved and pacified them with its harmonies", and then goes on to revise that opinion slightly: "Not resolved, really, or pacified, but, in Paul Alper's term, 'suspended in the harmonies of verse.'" And there is something about this account of the paradoxical relationship between the serenity of achieved form and "the hail of occurrence" that applies to the achievement of Michael Longley. Longley's usual tender inscription of flowers and crops is reminiscent of Virgil and the subtle, resistant strategies of the pastoral convention; but in 'Wounds' he manages to "suspend" the terrible material that occurs on every page of a book like *Northern Ireland: A Chronology of the Troubles* within the harmonies of his stately line and within an understanding available to him from his immediate family history.

Family history, a cherished landscape, inherited wounds, justified angers: all through the 60s John Montague's "poem including history" gathered and rooted itself in such concerns. *The Rough Field* (1972) shared with *Notes from the Land of the Dead* an ambition to find in the linked sequence a form that could suspend the particulars of a personal world within "the rough field/ of the universe/ growing, changing/ a net of energies/ crossing patterns/ weaving towards/ a new order." The work brought Montague to a point of visionary openness where his "plain sense of things" was at one with a larger architectonic, with the result that many of his subsequent lyrics (such as 'Small Secrets', from *A Slow Dance*,

1975) tremble not just with the delicacy of their own perceptions but with the background pressure of the rest of the oeuvre.

Concerns similar to those that drove John Montague to his native "rough field"—the *garbh achaidh* of Garvaghey—drove Michael Hartnett to return in the 70s to his home ground in Newcastle West and to the Irish language he had heard from his grandmother in childhood. *A Farewell to English* abounded in the paradoxes of the creative life: its author was setting out to kill the thing he loved, or rather love-hated, and yet at that very moment he was giving thrilling proof of how vividly the thing lived within him. 'Death of an Irishwoman' has all the turbulence and lucidity that drove Hartnett to his change of life and medium, but it also has a sureness of lyric touch that guaranteed his farewell to English would not be permanent. And Hartnett's work in the 70s had something else, something present also in the extravagant riffs and raves of Paul Durcan's volumes, a disappointment and impatience at the abdication and vacuities of public life in Euro-Ireland. These poets—and all the rest of the ones included here—meant business; the old Joycean rage for "the spiritual liberation of my country" was still alive and well, a rage which in Durcan's case got transformed into comedy, litany, the melody of panic and loss. Without prejudicing the essential seriousness of his endeavour, he told the reader, "The spoof will make you free."

I remember very well the moment when I felt Eavan Boland really meant business: I read her poem ("after Mayakovsky") called 'Conversation with the Inspector of Taxes about Poetry'—in *Hibernia,* I think—and felt the surge of things to come. Her determination to leave, as she says in the Preface to her *Collected Poems,* "the lighted circle and move out into the shadows of what I had learned to think of as an ordinary life" was electrically present in stanzas that took the language and the usual life by the scruff of the neck and shook it up in order to shake it down. The big compass of an 80s poem like 'The Journey' was already being described in the 70s air.

The three remaining poems were chosen because they represent bodies of work with very real but very different claims. Eiléan Ní Chuilleanáin and Pearse Hutchinson, both associated with *Cyphers* magazine, are poets with distinct aesthetics and highly individual styles, and don't fit neatly into any of the handy classifications. There is something second sighted, as it were, about Ní Chuilleanáin's work, by which I don't mean that she has any prophetic afflatus, more that her poems see things anew, in a rinsed and dreamstruck light. They are at once as plain as an anecdote told on the doorstep and as haunting as a soothsayer's greetings. Hutchinson's poems, on the other hand, are more like first footers, coming to the reader with personal news to tell, keeping him or her "in the presence of flesh and blood". In the 70s, his voice was heard regularly on RTÉ radio as presenter of a vigorous bilingual programme of words and music, and a poem 'Gaeltacht' springs from the same passion and forthrightness that characterized those broadcasts.

New Weather, the title of Paul Muldoon's first book, is taken from his poem 'Wind and Tree'. In the course of the decade, in books where virtuosity excelled itself and voice grew at once weightier and wilier, there are many more coruscating and complex lyric achievements, but none that mean more to me personally than this early poem which I saw before it was published and which I recognized—who wouldn't—as the work of one destined to traffic in delight and wisdom, to conjure readers and writers alike by the sound of sense and change their notions of what was what through the wise dream, as Borges called it, of artistic creation.

In a State of Flux (1980—1989)

Cathal Ó Searcaigh

*Words can't defeat Evil but they
can help us cope better with it*
— Franz Kafka

In a world severely threatened, now more than ever, with
unrestrained violence and relentless terrorism; ethnic strife and
bloodshed; ruthless tyrannies and oppressed multitudes; large
scale starvation and gratuitous destruction of our environment,
poetry sounds pointless. In these scary circumstances the word
"poetry" sounds shallow and a sham. But that's only if we cling
stubbornly to the snappy belief that poetry is the reserve of the
Academe—a highbrow curiosity, obscure and worthless—but not if
poetry is seen as a crucial medium of change, as a vital and an
eloquent instigator of meaning within society as a whole. And I stress
meaning because mankind requires meaning—or at least a search for
meaning—and poetry when it embodies its true calling is a quest for
meaning, for truth. Poetry at its best affirms lasting human values. It
confronts oppression. It opposes repression. Poems are always on the
side of light, always on the side of life. There is no higher religion,
according to the great Bengali poet, R. Tagore, than sympathy for all

that lives. Poetry, therefore, cannot and should not represent any collectivity or any superimposed set of values; the poet by defending his/her personal rights and independence is also defending every individual's rights and independence. The American poet Charles Olson's observations about filling our given space is, I think, a pertinent statement in this respect:

> ... a man; carved
> out of himself, so wrought he
> fills his given space, makes
> traceries sufficient to
> others needs ...
> here is
> social action, for the poet
> anyway, his
> politics, his
> needs ...

"To make traceries sufficient to others needs," as Olson endorses in his poem is, I think, an exemplary and effective role for the poet. In the profoundest sense it means to be politically aware. In these terrible times when man's inhumanity to man has grown to grotesque proportions, we all, poets included, must revere ourselves, recognise ourselves as life that wants to live among other forms of life that want to live. And isn't that what compassion is all about—an imaginative recognition of and a humane understanding towards all life forms. In these dehumanising days poetry needs to be compassionate, needs to care.

Faced by incoherence and chaos, by conspiracies against dignity and justice, poets have to summon a greater faith in human compassion than ever before, a stronger belief in human endurance to affirm love, to endorse truth. My choice of ten poems exemplify and express that belief. These poems, I believe, want to establish a redemptive, humane perspective in a world where such perceptions seem to have been blurred. These poems embody a heady mix of aesthetic complexity and social commitment, a new daring to address and challenge settled habits of style and an irrepressible boldness to defy stultifying social conventions. All of these poems pursue a genuine search for fresh meanings and methods, for authentic moments of faith and hope, for certain dependable continuities. They are concerned not only with the meaning of life but also with the life of meaning. They are about states of soul as much as they are about states of society. With their risky utterance and their urgency they are liberating rather than limiting.

Something of the spirit of the decade is, I hope, revealed in these poems. In the 80s Irish society was confused by social changes. There was a distinct rift—albeit a hesitant, ambivalent one—between church and state. The crozier no longer held sway in the Dáil, no longer transfixed the domestic. Assumptions that were once fixed and familiar were in an alarming state of flux. We were bewildered by the Kerry Babies scandal, shocked by the Ann Lovett tragedy, stunned by the Hunger Strikes. The economic slump depressed us. The exodus of our young unsettled us. Ireland of the 80s was more a state of absence than a place of presence. It was a void that was occasionally filled and enlivened by the holy commotion of the Moving Statues, by the high-spirited displays of the Soccer Squad, by the wild jolt of energy that was U2.

Trapped in their own helplessness, poets, like everybody else, can also develop an emotional and aesthetic fatigue. However, I think that the ten poets represented here responded to life in the Ireland of the 80s with creative eagerness and exuberance. They overcame the small-mindedness and the sordidness of the present by putting the immediate into a broader historical or mythical perspective. They seek shapes and figures, archetypal patterns that will allow them to confirm and clarify their own human experience, however tenuously, against a more resonant backdrop. Accustomed to discontinuities and discordancies, to ironies of identity, to self-doubt, some of them attempt to shift to a distant objective correlative the more pressing concerns of their poetry so that the aesthetic and ethical burdens of their lives will become a little bit more bearable, a little bit more understandable. They became adept at appropriating the irregular rhythms of life in the society around them to the private pressures of the psyche. They are "non-aligned storytellers" with an impulse toward the parable rather than the polemic.

All of these poets are familiar with the scathing tact and the dazzling shifts of subterfuge practised by the East European poets of the 60s and 70s. Under the hydra-headed monster of totalitarianism with its creepy censorship, Zbigniew Herbert in Poland, Miroslav Holub in Czechoslovakia, Vasko Popa in Yugoslavia, Marin Sorescu in Romania, all became connoisseurs of cogent irony, virtuosos of outspoken obliquities and well-versed masters of poetic double-talk. They astounded all of us who encountered them, even in translation, with the tightrope artistry of their poetries. In the face of ideological tyrannies and political correctness these poets carried a weighty moral sensibility, a deeply committed defence of humane values in times that enforced the depersonalisation of man.

The poets included here deploy some of the imaginative dexterity and the narrative cunning of these East European poets in their own handling of violent histories and deceitful politics. Heaney, Ó Dúill, McCarthy, Rosenstock, Carson, all draw upon historical anecdotes, potted histories and anecdotal personae that correspond somehow to their own politically embattled situations. Within their own experiences, their own emphases, they all bear witness to the tumult of our times. They are conscious of the fact that they inhabit history, that their various destinies are played out under its fierce eye; that their personal and particular histories coincide with a much broader history. Therefore, they are alert as an antenna to its signals. In Heaney's marvellous 'Terminus'—an eloquent and an enduring achievement, written it seems in response to the post-hunger strike stalemate—there is an austere amplitude. It is a poem that broadens the specific by giving it a mythical source and an epic scope, that is pitched beautifully between public utterance and private testimony. It is a poem about boundaries and borders, about tribal and political entrapment, about factions and frictions. But despite the disabling embitterments that bind it, it seems to me to be a poem that strives for or at least implies boundlessness. The ten poems I have selected represent man's spirit coming to terms with the anguish of being. They all aspire, either openly or covertly, to the redemptive and affirmative condition of boundlessness.

I would like to cast a cursory eye over the poetic careers of these ten poets during the 80s. That decade gave us the taut and elegant poems of Frank Harvey, a sadly neglected poet. Elegiac and lyric, regional and specific, true to their own world, they also open out wholeheartedly to other worlds. With their loops and links and whorls of sound, they vibrate in the memory with a profoundly mantric quality. The reinvented Ciaran Carson came forth in the 80s with his exquisitely fabricated, daringly digressive, thickly textured innovations and we witnessed the Irish lyric being opened up to more challenging and arresting modes of perceptions and reflections than it had ever attempted before.

We have the keenly perceptive chronicles of Thomas McCarthy, in which the thwarted ideals and misplaced hopes of the new Irish Republic are scrutinized and exposed in the hope, I assume, that some of this burdensome inheritance can be abandoned. Then, and only then, can we shape-up to new responsibilities, new futures. Eamon Grennan gave us his rapt contemplations of the commonplace, active meditations that ease us into alertness. We have in Eamon Grennan a true Seer, somebody who reveals the world anew. Reading his poems, we become more eye, more ear, more conscious of the momentousness of the ordinary. As a groundbreaking literary transgressor, Paul Durcan has been much lauded but much more castigated. But I hark back to Swift, "When a true genius appears you will know him by this sign, all the dunces are in a confederacy against him." In the 80s Durcan moved into an intensely creative spell. His best poems are savagely witty, heartbreakingly accurate documentaries of the changing social and sexual mores of the Ireland of our times. Dramatic monologues—

erotic, irreverent, delirious—that stomp and frolic between pastoral romance and full-frontal frankness. With the depth and intelligence of their insights, the integral and absolute humanity of their vision, these are poems to be cherished, to be revered, even. Nuala Ní Dhomhnaill, one of the essential voices of our times, came to prominence in the 80s. She is a poet with a world appeal and a world relevance. As we set forth on our voyage into the unknown millennium we need the visionary sorcery of her poems—the talismanic power of their revelations to steer us into safe havens, to light up our mortal days and nights. She is a poet of love, a loving poet. Her love extends to every blooming thing. Fauna and flora abound and bloom in her poems. Without this love, as Gary Snyder pointed out (and rightly so) we can end, even without war, with an uninhabitable planet. Her work is another splendid sample of what Máire Mhac an tSaoi characterised as "a living literature in a fast dying minority language."

Here, in her work and in the work of her gifted contemporaries, we hear the triumphant whoop of a threatened language which—despite the gloom and doom—is in these poems, alive to all the demands and the challenges of our century. Michael Davitt, a liberating force in Irish language poetry, published his *Selected Poems* in the late 80s. The jazzy urgency of his style made Gaelic go bebop in the night with a swinging, snazzy self-confidence. For a lot of us who came to poetry in the 70s and 80s he was the tuned-in, amped-up, street-wise cosmopolitan who set the fads, the lingo and the stances. His is an eloquent achievement, a record of richly human poems brought back from the edge of the abyss, from a zone of fear and desperation. Poems that make a tender appeal to the heart as they attempt to make sense of the world's grief and the soul's despair. In Gréagóir Ó Dúill's poems of the 80s, the instability of the self and the perishability of man amidst the upheavals of history is evoked with a fierce individualistic expressiveness. If Ó Dúill occasionally uses incongruities of expression or a more discordant diction it is because the existing resources of language become inadequate to his needs and he has to speak as an initiator, as an instigator of language. In this world of turmoil and transience, the poem, carved out with extreme difficulty, becomes a small illuminated moment of stability and truth. Gabriel Rosenstock's frame of reference is broader than that of any other poet writing in the Irish language at present. A poet who has assimilated much of what is best in world poetry, the range of his inventiveness is limitless. In the 80s he made wonder-voyages into Oriental realms of the imagination in search of emotional correlatives—plausible parallels from a remote historical past—that would allow him to make sense of the malaise of the present.

The four Irish language poems presented here are accompanied by translations. Gabriel Rosenstock, our greatest traveller across linguistic and cultural borders, said that translation was like a blood transfusion between friends. Frank Sewell, the most gifted poet of a new generation of Northern Ireland poets stated that the translator goes down on history; a cunning linguist. In this country, English and Irish have been colliding with each other for centuries; both physically and psychically. English poetry, I think, has benefited from and has been enriched by these encounters. Clarke, Kavanagh, Heaney, Montague, Muldoon, Carson, Meehan have all taken sustenance from the expressive energies of Irish. The ghost, the spectre of Irish, is continuously making an appearance in English language poetry in this country. It's like a poltergeist, upsetting the furniture of the poem, shuffling with the syntax, breathing through the metrics, uttering its own strange sounds. It's now time, I think, for Irish language verse to benefit from the scope and the range of English. I am delighted with the way that Frank Sewell has managed to invoke my own poems in English. He has found a voice and a register for them, that, seems to me to be acceptable in English. Likewise, Paul Muldoon and John Montague in particular, by deft and clever handling of tone and texture, have succeeded in making the poems of Michael Davitt and Nuala Ní Dhomhnaill speak in poetry and not in translationese. It just goes to prove, as somebody said, that poetry has many tongues but a single language.

Selecting ten poems to represent the decade is outrageously stingy. It's like trying to bake a cake using ingredients of only one syllable. Another ten would be equally niggardly but here they are, if only for the record: Derek Mahon's 'Ovid in Tomis'; Liam Ó Muirthile's 'An Parlús'; Dermot Bolger's 'Snuff Movies'; Michael O'Loughlin's 'Latin as a Foreign Tongue'; Paul Muldoon's 'The Sightseers'; Áine Ní Ghlinn's 'Gealt'; James Simmons's 'From the Irish'; Medbh McGuckian's 'Slips'; Biddy Jenkinson's 'Cáitheadh'; Eavan Boland's 'The Glass King'.

The flow goes on, a ripple in the rockpools here, a cascading torrent there. Sometimes breaking its banks, extending its limits; at other times languishing in backwaters. But always an outward flow, out to the ocean, unbounded. I will end with a Maori poem:

> From the family of mountains
> to the endless sea;
> I am the River
> the River is me.

Tidal Surge (1990—1999)

Nuala Ní Dhomhnaill

My earliest choice of the poems for this last decade of the century, and indeed the millennium, was sketched out in a rather desultory fashion at a table looking out over the idyllic scenery of Lake Bafa in the Aegean region of Turkey. As the sun set in the west and the moon rose almost simultaneously over the craggy peaks of Besparmak Dag, the ancient Mount Latmos, I could just make out at the lake's edge the ancient Sanctuary of Endymion, where I had once slept out during a night of a blue moon, hoping to incubate a dream worthy of a poet or at least a poem. I woke up hours later from a dreamless sleep, thinking that Keats would have made a better hand of it any time, and wishing that he could have made it as far as here instead of dying in two tiny rooms beside the Spanish steps in Rome. It was the perfect place to contemplate poems and poetry, made doubly so by the fact that I had absolutely no books at hand, and no other guidelines to go by other than the absolutely stern delineators of memory and emotional involvement, both of which served me rather well. The only question I asked myself in effect was "What are the poems that have left the strongest trace on me in the last ten years?"

Of course, I chose far too many poems. Speaking to Poetry Ireland on my subsequent return home I found out to my dismay

71

that *ten* meant just that exact number; no more and no less, and that for the practical purposes of this particular book, many of the poems I had chosen were much too long, and would have to be excerpted from or truncated, a surgical intervention I was loath to make, preferring my poems whole or not at all. So back to the drawing board, and another choice of poems, which was again easy to make, and if anything shows the great profusion of riches, the embarrassment of choice, that is available to anyone reading at all widely in contemporary Irish poetry. What you have actually happening is the continuing high-quality output of a great generation that came into print first in the 60s and 70s, including in the case of both Michael Longley and Derek Mahon, something of a comeback after what might be termed a fallow period, which though difficult for the individual poet at the time seems to me a necessary part of the process in terms of the long haul. "Ars est longissima via." It is the patience and doggedness to survive such necessary fallow periods that marks the true vocation of the poet. The old dog for the long road.

Add to this a later, but often overlapping generation that has come to maturity in the eighties and nineties, which includes the emergence "en masse" of womens' voices and which has caused what Eavan Boland has called "a different magnetic field" to emerge in Irish poetry. What has widened the field also is the acceptance, with the help of good translations, into the wider poetic community, of poets writing in Irish. This from what used to be a narrow "bantustan" in nothing less than a state akin to linguistic apartheid, where great voices such as Ó Ríordáin, Ó Direáin and Máire Mhac an tSaoi could be unknown and under-appreciated even by their contemporaries working in English. On top of this there is a new generation again, first published in the 90s, many of whom have written extremely good debut collections. So to put it mildly, the choice is mighty.

First of all though, a few words on the poems I had reluctantly to let go. John Montague's 'Border Sick Call', which finishes up his

Collected Poems (1995) is one of the great poems of the decade, lyrical and humane, encompassing in its scope both the salty pragmatism of the locals who actually live on the Border between North and South:

> Border be damned, it was a godsend,
> Have you ever noticed, cows have no religion?

and the more transcendental wisdom of his doctor-brother:

> but the real border is not between
> countries, but between life and death,
> that's where the doctor comes in.

It is a wonderful invocation of a land made strange by ice and snow, ending in a plaintive query which is very true of our time and place;

> But in what country have we been?

Another poem which it broke my heart to leave out, again mostly because of its length, was 'Incantata', by Paul Muldoon from *The Annals of Chile* (1994) as I think it is one of the high water-marks of our particular generation. (The equivalent perhaps for the previous generation of Derek Mahon's 'A Disused Shed in County Wexford'.) This poem is notorious in our house as the day I bought the book I had been out shopping for fresh prawns among other things. I came into the kitchen and left down the shopping bags beside the table, and flicked—as I thought— momentarily through the book, only to be totally mesmerized by this poem. Witness the dismay of the rest of the family when they returned home three hours later to find me still glued to the poem at the table, reading it over and over again, totally unaware of the overwhelming stink of decomposition as prawns and other perishables went off in the heat so that they had to be all thrown out. The trials of those who live with poets ...

Another poem that I am truly sorry not to have been able to include because ten is only and could only be ten, is Eavan Boland's 'That the Art of Cartography is Limited' (*In a Time of Violence*, 1994) because it is a beautiful and truly lyrical evocation of one of the great silences that until recently have hung over both the Irish landscape and our collective psyche, that of the Great Famine. I trusted in any case that Eavan would be well represented in the selections from the previous decades, as she has been publishing since the 60s. An omission that will strike many as even more strange is that of any poems by our Nobel Laureate of the 90s, Seamus Heaney. I still remember the over-whelming delight of that September day in 1995 when, working at my desk, with Raidió na Gaeltachta on, I heard on their midday news flash that Seamus Heaney had won the Nobel prize. It seemed so totally his due, as he has been one of the most committed and sustained and sustaining of Irish poets since his early début in the 60s. There are many poems that I really love in his work since he gained the prize, especially three from *The Spirit Level:* 'Saint Kevin and the Blackbird', because of its wonderful evocation of myth and the role of story and metaphor; the thin tight lines of 'Cassandra' which touch on the tough topic of sex and guilt in a way maybe not seen in this poet since *North;* and the wonderful technical pizzazz of the sestina 'Two Lorries', which barely holds in through its technical virtuosity a heavy payload of pain and grief. Nevertheless, and at the risk of something akin to pure perversity, I have omitted this our greatest senior poet from my choice of the 90s, knowing him to be more than **well** represented in every decade from the 60s onwards, and in **an attempt** to try and make room for some new poets in what **has grown** gradually through the decades into a bewildering profusion of different voices. And by that I don't mean Paddy Kavanagh's specious standing army of ten thousand either, but rather a very serious array of big guns who can take their place with anyone and in any international arena.

Now for the actual poems I *did* choose. 'Marconi's Cottage', from the book of that title, is as nearly typical a poem as I could find of Medbh McGuckian's multi-levelled and multifarious oeuvre, which has been as rich in its development in the 90s as it was in the 80s, culminating in her new book *Shelmalier* based (as much as any poem of Medbh's is based) on the Rebellion of 1798. If anybody has most changed the "territories of the voice" of Irish poetry in recent times, that person has to be Medbh. A dense secretive inner world unfolds in poems of great and subtle rhythmical and imagistic beauty. As Ciaran Carson wrote in a recent issue of *Verse* (Volume 16, number 2): "There is no one like McGuckian writing in the English language, and we should be grateful for her ornate and ambiguous presence. Too often, I have been asked, 'But what does it all mean?' You might as well ask what Charlie Parker 'means'. He means music. McGuckian means poetry and as she puts it in *Shelmalier,* 'This great estrangement has the destination of a rhyme.'"

Another major female voice from the 90s has been Paula Meehan and her poem 'The Pattern' has already taken on the status of a classic. A richly textured evocation of a childhood growing up in Dublin's inner city and the deeply ambiguous relationship between mother and daughter are explored throughout the poem but best summed up in its final lines:

> Tongues of flame in her dark eyes,
> she'd say, 'One of these days I must
> teach you to follow a pattern.'

Another classic poem about the mother/daughter relationship is Eiléan Ní Chuilleanáin's 'Fireman's Lift'. Though ostensibly a description in precise detail of the painting of the *Ascension of the Virgin Mary* painted by Correggio on the great Renaissance copula that sits rather incongruously on top of the otherwise Romanesque structure of the Cathedral of Parma, it is also an elegy to her mother, who was standing beside her when she first saw it. An immense act of grieving, the poem itself is perhaps a translation of the mother's image in the older, medieval, and religious sense of the word as transformation, or removal from earth into heaven. "Tell the truth but tell it slant", was Emily Dickinson's dictum and I think that one of the great strengths of Irish poetry in our time is a necessary reticence in the face of the personal, a refusal to follow the straight in-your-face confessional mode which, fuelled originally by TV sound-bites, has come to dominate most of the art forms of our time, including, sad to say, much of modern American poetry. I say unfortunately, because, though it has its moments, ultimately its very topicality and closeness to the facts of any particular individual's life leaves it very one-dimensional and often trite. I know I am going against the spirit of the age, which is that of the apotheosis of the memoir, but unless the commonplace details of our lives are shot through by something of more permanence, our poems are built on sand, and on them we can build no lasting city.

This Irish preference for obliqueness and the great artistic advantages to be gained by speaking of the personal and the here and now through an "objective correlative" or a distancing lens of some kind is best exemplified by one of the great poems of the 90s, Michael Longley's 'Ceasefire'. Though collected in his 1994 volume *The Ghost Orchid,* it made its first electrifying appearance in print in *The Irish Times* to coincide with the announcement by the IRA of the first Northern Ireland ceasefire. Though Michael assures me it was written sometime before and appeared then purely as a fluke, I myself am not too sure of that, John Banville being the Literary Editor of the paper at the time. He knew what he had here, and he was right; its effect was dynamic, and rippled right through the community, both North and South, having a galvanizing effect that can only be imagined of some lines of Yeats, perhaps, at the turn of the century—the "Did you see an old woman go down the road", of 'Kathleen Ní Houlihan' or the "terrible beauty is born" of 'Easter 1916'. Trusting the words of the Odyssey to speak to us through the ages Longley has Priam sigh:

'I get down on my knees and do what must be done
And kiss Achilles' hand, the killer of my son'

lines which have been taken to heart by many on this island and are among those most quoted in conversation or in print during this last decade.

Which brings me to one of the reasons I chose my next poem, Cathal Ó Searcaigh's 'Gort na gCnámh' or 'The Field of Bones' as it is translated by Frankie Sewell. This first appeared in Irish alone in a book called *Na Buachaillí Bána* (1996), which was among many other things Cathal's testament of "coming out" in terms which could not by a long shot be called uncertain. Nevertheless the poem in the book that caused the most commotion is not about homosexuality at all, but rather the description of the dire straits of a young woman violated by her father who had to suffocate and bury her newborn child in the eponymous "Field of Bones". This poem caused an absolute furore in Cathal's home place and caused him amongst other things, to be "read out from the altar"; in other words a sermon was preached against him, a social punishment which in my innocence I had thought had gone out with the proverbial Flood. I heard him subsequently defending himself on Raidió na Gaeltachta with both dignity and aplomb, and it seems from all appearances that he came off the winner in this particular verbal duel. The days when a poor Tailor could be forced to burn a book of his own harmless, witty, and hilarious reminiscences (*The Tailor and Ansty* by Eric Cross) have at long last been superseded. Still, that the very attempt was made to pillory Cathal over this poem is to me actually a great sign, proof positive that poetry in Ireland is still taken with a seriousness that it has lost out on in most Western societies, and maybe most especially in

America. The other Irish language poem that I have chosen 'Tuireamh Marie Antoinette', could hardly be more different in many ways to Cathal's poem, but in its "bricolage" of some curious historic facts, European sophistication and a personal history of a young Irish girl's innocence, wonder, and subsequently incongruous confusion about what on earth breasts are all about, it is brave and venturesome, and dares to push out to the very extremities the limits and definitions of what is possible in a poem in Irish. Biddy Jenkinson, in line with a long-held and morally impeccable policy, is not willing to have her poem translated into English in Ireland.

Peter Sirr's work to me does the same for poetry in Ireland in English. Having digested the best of what American poetry has to offer, here, in his fourth collection *The Ledger of Fruitful Exchange*, he really comes into his own. The poem I would have most liked to have chosen from this collection is the (very long) 'A Journal', a very moving and technically brilliant variation on that great perennial theme in poetry, the growth and the death of love, but its length barred it from the limits of this book, and I would consider it nothing short of barbaric to chip and chop at it. Therefore I accepted as compromise 'Trade Songs', not just for its exotic splendours, but because in its espousal of the best of American techniques, it makes a welcome change from the perpetually inward and often futile navel-gazing which is a constant risk in Irish poetry.

In a sense, through the sheer volume of his production both in poetry and prose, the 90s is the decade of Ciaran Carson. Having hit his stride with the long line in the late 80s with *The Irish for No* and *Belfast Confetti* he has continued the run with *First Language, Opera Et Cetera, The Twelfth of Never, HMS Belfast,* not to mention three prose non-fiction books, *Last Night's Fun, The Star Factory* and *Fishing for Amber.* Again the sheer choice of poems is prodigious but with my constant awareness of the sub-stratum of Irish that underlies even his most colourful displays of English fireworks, I could not help but be completely seduced by 'Eesti', where the sepia-coloured nostalgia of an afternoon in Tallinn, the capital of Eesti or Estonia brings him back to a red-letter day in his youth and his father's admonition in Irish to "Éist", which means at the same time both "Listen" and "Be silent".

Nothing delights me more in the poetry of the 90s than the resurrection of Derek Mahon, albeit so far only in rhyming couplets. After much consideration of many fine poems in *The Hudson Letter* and *The Yellow Book* I finally decided on 'To Eugene Lambe in Heaven', as my favourite. I never met Eugene Lambe personally, though I have heard a lot about him from many quarters. But this doesn't make a whit of difference, as this poem makes me think I knew the man, so subtly and completely is he rounded out before us. The last line too, haunts me and is one that I have heard myself whisper at odd moments, either climbing the stairs to bed or stalled at Dublin traffic lights:

Oft in the stilly night I remember our wasted youth.

And finally, but only chronologically last—if we do not take into consideration the wedding-feast at Cana—the poem that I chose instead of 'Incantata', is 'Long Finish' by Paul Muldoon from his 1998 collection, *Hay*. This double "ballade" encompasses everything from the necessary address to the "Princess of Accutane" in the last verse which is typical of and necessary to the original form, to a meditation on ten years of married life, and from there it takes off to some of the awful things that have happened in Northern Ireland during that period, and then returns by way of a digression through Japanese literature and the reality of waking up in Japan, to the virtues of married life, "and then some".

I have this poem pinned up beside my writing desk. I am deeply envious of it. So much so that every time I look up it spurs me on to try again, another poem, or at least another stab at one. In its extraordinary technical virtuosity and depth of heart it sums up everything that I consider valuable in Irish poetry in the 90s.

I am sorry I have not been able to make more room for the admirable new generation of those such as David Wheatley, Justin Quinn, Vona Groarke, Mary O'Malley, Rita Ann Higgins, Moya Cannon, Enda Wyley, Sinéad Morrissey, Kerry Hardie and others, some of whom have followed up remarkable debut collections with very good seconds. Given the wide range of this river of song as it reaches the end of a hundred years, God forgive me for having acquiesced to choosing only ten poems for the last decade in the first place.

TWO

Twentieth-Century Irish-Language Poetry

Theo Dorgan

A t the dawn of the twentieth century, borne up on the rising tide of national feeling, nurtured by the Gaelic League's recuperative work on the poetry of the past, an Irish-speaking optimist might have predicted a flood of new poetry in the language as a feature of the coming times. He, or she, would have been both incautious and destined to be disappointed. The first Gaelic poet of serious achievement in the new century, Máirtín Ó Direáin, would not even begin to think of writing poetry in Irish until 1938, and would say at the outset *"Níor chabhair mhór d'éinne againn san aois seo aon uaill ná mac alla ó na filí a chuaigh romhainn inár dteanga féin"*—No cry or echo from the poets who went before us in our own tongue would be of help to any of us in this time.

Apart from Ó Direáin, no poetry of true value would appear in the Irish language until Seán Ó Ríordáin published *Eireaball Spideoige* in 1952. Consumptive, lonely and unillusioned, Ó Ríordáin was a kind of alienated pietist whose work strikes the first truly modern note in Gaelic poetry. Refusing the succour of sentimental loyalty to the forms and tropes of the high Gaelic tradition, his agonised soul-searching is a local version of the doubt and existential anguish which now seems so characteristic of the European mid-century. But Ó Direáin's reluctant, even angry abandoning of the Arcadian peasant dream does not quite make him modern, in the sense that Eoghan Ó Tuarisc, say, writing self-consciously under the shadow of the Bomb, is modern. Paradoxically, Máire Mhac an tSaoi, immersed as she is in the poet-scholar tradition, becomes modern precisely because of her ability to play off a distinctly independent and contemporary sensibility against the structures and strictures of inherited traditions. Seán Ó Tuama, with his Corkman's ancestral yearning for the Mediterranean, and Pearse Hutchinson, drawn to Galicia and Catalonia, find distinctive contemporary voices in Irish outside the sway of world-girdling English; one might say the same of Tomás Mac Síomóin, heavily and productively indebted to a Continental sensibility which owes more to Pasolini than to Pearse.

Caitlín Maude, who died tragically young, and Michael Hartnett, to whom we will return, both born in 1941, carry the mid-century: the fomer as a feminist *avant la lettre*, the latter as a gifted poet in both Irish and English, translator of Ó Bruadair, eidetic companion to the present generation even in death. Maude and Hartnett, as with the generation following swiftly on their heels, were more of the present moment than of Ireland, in the important sense that the Gaelic world was for them a repository of enormous resource for the living of a life, far more than it was a heavy and inescapable ancestral burden. They and their successors are of post-Catholic, post nationalist Ireland, the Ireland that was beginning to struggle to its feet at about the time they began publishing their youthful verses.

If the Gaelic League had, as it were, an afterlife following the establishment of the Irish Free State it was not vivifying, but the reverse. We can see it now as an admirable project of recovery and recuperation which carried within itself the metal fatigue of Victorian sentimentalism. The lost Gaelic order towards which it flung out a bridge was aristocratic, disdainful, Catholic and doomed. Apt in and for its time, the poetry of that order was spectacularly ill-suited to the grubby, dour, post-colonial truth of the infant Republic which would seize on it as the epitome of native high culture and, by force-feeding it in the schools, rob it of its political charge while unconsciously undermining its power as art. The insular, primitive nationalism of the new ruling class seized on the rich poetry of the 17th and 18th centuries as a shining string of baubles, the pathetic jewels of the poor who do not recognise their own poverty nor understand where their true wealth is to be found. By resolutely closing out the modern in favour of an idealised and unreal nexus of virtuous peasant and cultured Lord, the State, through its 'education' system, made the disjunction between a glorious poetry of the past and a possible poetry of the present both absolute and prescriptive. Seeking, for perhaps the best motives, to celebrate the high poetry of a comparatively recent past, it silenced the present.

There were, to be sure, disruptions. Frank O'Connor, no cherished treasure of the State, published a muscular translation of *Cúirt an Mheán-Oíche, The Midnight Court*, in 1945, followed by *Kings, Lords and Commons* and *A Golden Treasury of Irish Poetry 600- 1200* (with David Greene), both in 1959. These books, paradoxically, awakened his English language readers to the intrinsic riches of the Gaelic poetic tradition, and helped make it possible to see in a positive context work which, unfortunately, the State had helped stigmatise as backward and unworthy of serious attention.

There were disruptions, and there was also a nourishing silence. Away from the eyes of the State and the new professional class of Gaeilgeoirí, in "unforgiven places" as Tony Curtis puts it, Irish continued to be spoken as a living, adaptive and ambitious language. On building sites in Coventry as much as in the botháns of Kerry and the fire stations of Boston and Chicago, with neither fuss nor fanfare, the language endured and mutated, as all living languages do, out of sight and out of mind. There is nobody more secretively rebellious than a man or woman who is assured by the well-off that poverty is an admirable thing; nothing is better suited to the life of a language than the secrecy of the poor; and nothing more appeals to a rebel than a language in which to access simultaneously both a hidden past and an unborn future. The rebels, as it happens, were waiting in the wings.

When Nuala Ní Dhomhnaill and Michael Davitt, Gabriel Rosenstock and Liam Ó Muirthile arrived in University College Cork, they were coming to themselves as poets in what Che Guevara, in a different context but at more or less the same time, described as "an objectively revolutionary situation". They would found, and be published in, a radical journal, INNTI.

The power of the State to contain reality had withered. The electronic age and the first world generation were upon us, rock and roll had thundered out across the world and the short-lived counter culture, for a dizzy moment, held the commanding heights. The first trans-national generation had arrived to claim its place in the sun, and considerably to the surprise of the tweeds and Fáinne brigade this brash and exuberant generation of poets was as unremarkably at home in the Gaeltachts as in the hip, wide world.

Nuala Ní Dhomhnaill, born in Lancashire, brought up in Nenagh and in the Gaeltacht of Corcha Dhuibhne, was a natural rebel with a profound sense of the riches of the folk tradition, as source both of story and syntax. Michael Davitt, son of a C.I.E worker, and Liam Ó Muirthile from the heart of Cork City found themselves wildly at home in the Gaeltachts of Corcha Dhuibhne and Cúil Aodha, party and privy to a racy reality the pietists of the language had ignored or tried to forget. There was a true exuberance in the air, perhaps more soberly shared by Gréagóir Ó Dúill and Micheal O'Siadhail (his own preferred spelling) in other places, a sense that, as John Montague put it, "old moulds are broken" and that a new world, a new language was both possible and necessary. An Irish language, to put it this way, that could contain LSD and Gabriel Rosenstock's abiding faith in the wisdom-literature of the East.

The wily and sceptical Seán Ó Tuama offered a bracing counterpoint to their wilder enthusiasms, perhaps, as Seán ó Riada brought a demonic precision to the music he did so much to uncover and make new again, in the same place and at the same time, but for all that, the INNTI poets were essentially unruly and individual as much as they were ever a school. Their education helped shape but does not explain them.

They were excoriated as shallow barbarians, dabblers in the shallows of the language, polluters of the unsullied, sex-free, drug-free paradise of the Gael. Contemptuous of the carefully-nurtured and comfortable state-within-a-state which the professional Gaeilgeoirí had so profitably and quietly nurtured, they earned, in some quarters, genuine, spitting hatred. It is true that their focus was on the immediate, the lyric instant of the body present to itself, the street as theatre of the present moment, the exalted state of mind as both norm and normative. In that sense they were very much of their time, in fact so much of their time that, disconcertingly, they were of the avant-garde in a way that few of their English-language contemporaries were. Formally and thematically, they were ripping through received forms and received wisdom in unprecedented ways; perhaps only Paul Durcan, at that time, was doing in English what these poets were doing in Irish. This cleavage with the past, especially with the immediate past, was so shocking that, in effect, the shock anaesthetised itself. They were out and through into a new, unexpected re-appropriation of the past almost before they, themselves, realised what was going on.

It should be noted that the rising generation of poets were both heartened and inspired to a more capacious sense of their inheritance by the visits to Ireland of Scottish Gaelic poets, singers and musicians organised by Colonel Eoghan Ó Néill, and by the reciprocal visits to Scotland which would enter into the folklore as well as the poetry. The sense of a cognate tradition and of a comradeship in struggle became and remains an amplification and a quickening of commitment to the language, to a life in the language.

We live in a changed landscape now. Biddy Jenkinson can forge, as she has done, a lapidary and rigorous language of her own, steeped in the cold water of the language, and be and feel free to do so. Áine Ní Ghlinn can dare her poems to the edge of cold prose, write of the most painful things, and occasion no reproach that she lacks the classical frame of reference. Cathal Ó Searcaigh, whose beginning was in Kerouac, whose delight is in an unabashed

gay sensibility, can write of Nepal and Gort 'a Choirce and sex
satisfactory and unsatisfactory and know he will be read and heard
as a poet of the living moment. These things are true, and
remarkable. Colm Breathnach and Louis de Paor are the first of the
post INNTI generations, each a true and individual poet, each
lyrical and intelligent in his individual way. Both of them are born
into a new kind of liberty—as, indeed, is the gifted Belfast poet,
Gearóid Mac Lochlainn—for they can now include among their
forebears men and women who crafted a new ethos and a new
sense of what is possible for Irish poetry in our time, and for even
younger poets in the time that is to come.

The cleavage is absolute between our now and our past, insofar
as that past was constructed as an ideal reservation without whose
walls there could be no salvation. The cleavage is, also, an illusion:
language comes down to us as a living stream, defying all efforts to
shape and contain its course. It is literally not possible to engage
with the present of a language, to write in a language, without being
informed by the past of that language. What is different is that the
poet today can pick and choose where to immerse herself in the
past, can come to the past as part of the project of making his own,
unique existential self as a poet. There is an essential freedom in this
relationship to the past, a freedom which is at base a kind of
absolute humility and without which there can be no genuine
respect for the life and work of those who have gone before us.

When Michael Hartnett, Mícheál Ó hAirtnéide, came "with
meagre gifts to court the language of my people", when he turned
from English to Irish, to his own immediate present as well as the
living present of Ó Bruadair and Ó Rathaille, it was a gesture read
in one of two ways: it was quixotic and arbitrary, or it was a choice
made in the face of forces, a-historical powers, he was helpless to
resist. With the passage of time, and following his uncriticised and
civilly-received return to English, it is possible now to see that
Hartnett's choice was made in response to a simple imperative: the
words sought him out, and the words were in Irish.

And this, I think, is where we are now. When poets now living
make their poems in Irish, they are making poems, not obeisances,

not signs made in the name of a tradition but the elements themselves of a free, living tradition. Poems. In Irish. No more, and no less.

This essay originally appeared in *An Leabhar Mór / The Great Book of Gaelic,* edited by Malcolm Maclean and Theo Dorgan, produced by Proiseacht Nan Ealan and first published by Canongate Books in 2002. It was reissued by the O'Brien Press, Ireland, in 2008.

The American Connection:
An Influence on Modern
and Contemporary Irish Poetry

EAMON GRENNAN

There were a number of ways of approaching this subject—the relationship between Irish and American poetry. Specific themes and issues, for example: time and space; the way history is present to both poetries; how Irish and American poets deal (differently) with their respective geographies. Or the connection in both countries between poetry and politics (how poems by Kinsella or Montague or Heaney or Boland or Muldoon—in which some explicit or implicit political pressure may be felt stirring, shaping, sensitising the material—might compare with poems by Kinnell or Levertov or Simic or Hass). The related issue of community edged into a question: is there a distinct sense of *community* within the work of many Irish poets (in spite of what Kinsella has said about "scattering of incoherent lives"),[1] while it is a palpable absence in recent American poetry? The notion of faith (in what?) in a broad sense was another beguiling possibility, throwing open the Pandora's can of worms of "secular" imagination and some other kind: the figuring of immanence and transcendence in the poetic firmaments of the two countries. The status of Irish and American poetry—both "post-colonial," but *how*, precisely—*vis-à-vis* the English tradition (in general or from

90

the more limited point of view of Romanticism) was also a topic worth investigating. Aside from all these, there were the more strictly *formal* possibilities: poetic use of the English language in 20th Century Irish and American verse, for example; or a comparison between the way an Irish poem and an American poem actually conduct themselves on the page (as seen, perhaps, in a passage of Whitman and one of Yeats, something by Kavanagh and by Williams, a piece by Kinsella set beside one by Ashbery or some Jorie Graham, a Heaney poem beside a poem by Pinsky, one by Ní Chuilleanáin alongside one by Plath, something by James Merill next to a few stanzas of Derek Mahon).

Having considered such possible subjects, however, I found myself thinking more about a simpler and more straightforwardly historical issue: the way, if at all, American poetry of the past century has nourished the body of Irish poetry in English during that time. Such an exploration, more fundamental than the others I've mentioned, could serve as a base or preliminary study for them. This, accordingly, became the topic of the following essay.

I was first awakened to a tangible connection between Irish and American poetry during a reading given by Thomas Kinsella at Vassar College, in 1974 or '75. Kinsella spoke of his own emancipation as a poet being due to the enabling influence of William Carlos Williams. "Doctor Williams," as Kinsella insisted on calling him, freed him from the restrictions of the iambic line and offered him by example the possibilities of a new music. When I asked Kinsella to read 'A Country Walk' for my class in Irish Literature, he baffled them by bemoaning its limp iambics, and would only read it under protest. He also spoke of Pound, of the *Cantos* as exemplary poetic action, praising their inclusiveness and their enigmas. It was no harm, he explained, for a reader to have to *work* at a poem; no harm to be compelled to discover some new facts, the actual meaning of some esoteric allusion or scrap of mandarin Chinese. Such a fit reader, it has struck me since, is precisely the reader Kinsella himself hopes for, a ready traveller in those often bewildering realms of personal and cultural history which his poetry since *Nightwalker* has opened up.

Since that time I've been aware of the American influence as a real presence in the work of contemporary Irish poets. It is not hard to support such a feeling. John Montague, for example, has often voiced his debt to poets like Ransom and Creeley and Robert Duncan. Seamus Heaney's year in Berkeley (1970-71) not only introduced him to the poetry of Duncan and Snyder and Bly, and the meshing of cultural, political and mythological frames of reference it managed, but led also to "a release I got just by reading American poetry, in particular coming to grips with Carlos Williams", and to "a more relaxed movement to the verse".[2] All this on top of the touches of Frost, Roethke, and Lowell that can be found in and between his lines. In Eavan Boland's recent poetry it is hard not to hear cadences, detect images, recognise language, feel the pressure of attitudes which must owe something to Sylvia Plath and Adrienne Rich, while Paul Muldoon's dazzling displays of eccentric ventriloquism reveal an imaginative hospitality to a whole spectrum of American poets, from Frost to Berryman, Pound and Stevens, to Ashbery and Charles Simic. Michael Longley, too, would hardly deny a drop of Emily Dickinson or John Crowe Ransom among his civil stanzas, and Derek Mahon could probably stand to be told that traces of Stevens, Lowell, and Pound were detectable among his. And in the idiosyncratic, vatic and comic voices of Paul Durcan it may be possible to hear echoes of Ginsberg and Ferlinghetti. Approximate as they may be, I suspect most readers would find themselves roughly in agreement with these claims, all of which add up to the simple fact that modem and contemporary American poetry has had a strong, substantial influence on the poetry at present being written in Ireland.

What, however, of the past? The subject of this paper forced me to consider the sources of such influence, to wonder how far back it went, what its history might be, or its meaning. What follows is a preliminary sketch of the territory opened up by such questions. As usual, it's necessary to start with Yeats. At first it may seem odd, but then right, that the young man who in March 1887 sat in a house in Harold's Cross and dreamt of starting "a school of Irish poetry" could reveal to an anonymous correspondent his belief that

"Whitman is the greatest teacher of these decades".[3] A teacher, as it later appears, of cultural nationalism, and so a natural model for the young Yeats. And since Whitman is "very American," even though "America was once an English colony," it follows of necessity that "it should be easy for us, who have in us that wild Celtic blood, the most unEnglish of all things under heaven, to make such a literature".[4] To this explicitly nationalist and ideological stimulus, Yeats added his heightened sense of Whitman as the poet-as-outcast, at odds with his society, "neglected and persecuted," hounded by moralists in spite of being "the most National of her poets," and the victim (as Yeats would in time come to see himself) of an "uneducated and idle" public.[5] In such a role (a sort of literary Parnell), as well as in his role as teacher, Whitman is to Yeats something like what Ibsen is to the young Joyce. He alerts the Irish poet not only to the possibilities of creating a new literature, but to the concomitant need (central to the Revival) to create an audience for that literature.

Beyond ideology and image, Yeats must also have felt the stylistic pressure of Whitman. The poet who would in time refer to his poems as "my true self" must surely have been struck by the emphatic revelation of personality in the work of the American. In fact, Whitman's "he who touches this book touches a man" is in 1892 a term of praise in Yeats's critical writing.[6] And by citing with approval the "wild irregular verses of Todhunter's 'Banshee' as a cross "between Walt Whitman and the Scotch Ossian," Yeats almost manages to turn the American into an honorary Celt.[7] Finally, that *Leaves of Grass* is so vigorously a *speaking* book, a book of impassioned speech ("my own voice," says Whitman, "orotund sweeping and final")[8], must have been a conscious or unconscious encouragement to a poet eager "to make the language of poetry coincide with that of passionate, normal speech".[9] By a fine irony of literary history, then, what Yeats will come to see as the particular, civilised distinction of his case—"Gradual Time's last gift, a written speech / Wrought of high laughter, loveliness and ease"—owed something in its beginnings to a barbaric Transatlantic yawp.[10]

Whitman is not the end of Yeats's connection with the American muse. Ezra Pound came first (to Europe) to learn from Yeats. Being Pound, he ended up teaching the older poet a thing or two.[11] In a sense, Pound—who called Whitman "a pig-headed father," but also acknowledged "We have one sap and one root" (how Yeats, in his despairing search for a literary father, must have envied such assured kinship)—begins American literature for the second time. It seems natural enough, then, that Pound should help Yeats re-make himself, begin again. Not only did he give Yeats a less eccentric view of literary history (convincing him that between the Greeks and Elizabethans there was more than "a great blank"), he also urged his verse towards something sparer, harder, more aggressively present to that world, "harsher and more outspoken".[12] In addition to the fact that the two poets met around 1909, such qualities (seen in *The Green Helmet* and *Responsibilities)* suggest that Pound's influence took over where that of Synge was broken off by Synge's death (March, 1909). Pound's own comments on these two volumes echo, I would imagine, Yeats's feeling about the new elements in his verse. They contain, says Pound in a review, "a manifestly new note"; they have "prose directness"; they show "his work becoming gaunter, seeking greater hardness of outline".[13] Yeats's own view of Pound, uttered shortly after their first meeting, suggests the sort of benefits he would reap from his contact with "this queer creature".[14] Pound is close "to the right sort of music for poetry," he says to Lady Gregory, "music with strongly marked time and yet it is effective speech".[15]

Where Whitman, then, was one of Yeats's important teachers in the establishment of his first poetic self, Pound taught him to re-make himself and move towards the style of his maturity, during a time when he "thought that anything good in poetry would come out of America".[16] It seems fitting, therefore (as well as another ironic twist in the thread of literary history), that it has often been Pound and later American heirs of Whitman who have assisted more recent Irish poets to free themselves from the power- (or prison-) house of Yeats—the rich, seductive, varied magniloquence of the mature and later verse.

Although Louis MacNeice wrote a book about modern poetry, and although like everyone else in the Thirties he undoubtedly felt the influence of Eliot, and although he actually lived and taught in America before the war, he shows little interest in or knowledge of American poetry. And what he does know he seems negative about. Among other things, he distrusts the spirit of Whitman, whose optimism offends him and whose tendency to formal excesses ("a wrong-headed attempt at spontaneity")[17] threatens MacNeice's own (more or less rationalist) bias towards common sense. He punctures Pound's Imagist manifesto at every point, and objects to the method of the *Cantos* because their "passion for the particular detail conduces to a total blur".[18] When he comes to write a long poem of his own *(Autumn Sequel)* in what one might think could have been an American, loose-limbed manner, he is at pains to insist his model is Spenser, not the *Cantos*. Nor does he have anything good to say about Ransom ("a dainty contemplative whimsicality, centered on domestic objects," that "brought a metaphysical attitude into the nursery"), or cummings (nothing but "tough-guy sentimentality").[19]

Such a wholesale lack of sympathy is probably due to MacNeice's own search for some sort of contemporary common-sense classicism. From such a point of view (sharpened by a certain Northern canniness and restraint), American poetry has to seem a stew of excesses: excesses of emotion ("sentimentality"), of openness ("wrong-headed spontaneity"), of particularity ("blur"), and of craft ("whimsicality"). What the undeniably vital principle of Whitman (with whom he yoked D.H. Lawrence) needed, argued MacNeice, was to be properly *girdered* "with a structure supplied partly by reason, partly by emotion intelligently canalised to an end, partly by the mere love of form".[20] Terms such as these—added to the fact that MacNeice probably didn't *need* American poetry because he felt comfortable with the classics, the English tradition, and a comparatively limited ("traditional") sense of the meaning of "form"—ensure that the poets of America don't ever truly enter the bloodstream of MacNeice's verse. Why this should remain a somewhat surprising fact is because what he says of Whitman and Lawrence ("poetry keeping pace with their lives and with their beliefs as affecting their lives")[21] could be applied, though in a different *formal* spirit, to some of his own intentions as a poet.

As with just about everything else in Austin Clarke's career, his connection with American poetry is oblique, occluded, enigmatic. Given his explicit commitment to the "Irish Mode" and his early relationship to the Revival and Revivalism, it is a surprise to find Americans at the very source and opening of Clarke's imaginative life as a poet. While these early influences may seem, in the larger picture, slight enough, they are nonetheless worth mentioning.

After what he calls his "experiences of nature", it was Longfellow's *Hiawatha* which first awakened the poet in Clarke, giving him his "first experience of the evocative power of verbal rhythm".[22] In stylistic terms this may not have been a particularly "American" experience, but there was also, to judge by a comparatively late poem, an early encounter with Whitman. It is in 'Old Fashioned Pilgrimage' (written after the pivotal *Mnemosyne Lay in Dust,* which had emancipated his memory and given him the freedom of his whole past) that Clarke recalls his startled early discovery of Whitman:

> I heard his free verse come
> In a rhythmic run of syllables that spread around me, loud
> And soft … I was a
> Boy, turning that once forbidden book, *The Leaves*
> *Of Grass,* word-showered, until my body was naked and self-proud
> As I looked it boldly up and down, vein-ready, well stocked;
> Joy rising.[23]

Whitman is here vividly connected with Clarke's discovery of his own sexuality. And since Clarke's sexuality is so bound to his imagination, to his life as a poet—either in celebratory, satiric, or desperate ways—Whitman's forbidden book can be reasonably associated with Clarke's growth into and as a poet, even his discovery of a sort of verbal Eden, innocent and extravagantly sensual. Beyond the auto-erotic intensity of this response to *Leaves of Grass,* the connection with Whitman is further endorsed by Clarke's awareness of the American poet's passionate commitment to a common social being, his image of universal fraternity, of "Europe, America, Asia, Africa together".[24] In Clarke's own case, on the other hand, it is the blunting of precisely these sexual and social possibilities (more specifically understood on his terms) that hurt him into poetry. So Whitman's exemplary nature is, for Clarke, suggestive of some Paradise Lost of human freedom.

Later than the encounter with Whitman, Clarke's experience of Poe is also, however, crucial to his development as a poet. So, at least, it would seem from 'Old Fashioned Pilgrimage,' in which he also visits the shrine of Poe's "small white cottage." A dream reveals the way Poe's poetry was implicated in the most sexually traumatic circumstance of Clarke's young manhood. Poe's romantic fever of desire is a disease Clarke feels he himself suffered from, most notably in the unconsummated affair with "Margaret", known from the autobiography, *Mnemosyne,* and from some curious intrusions into the early epics.[25] It was this condition ("Cornelia, in the candlelight, uneasy / With love, thin pallor and gloom, under her nightgown, half seen") that drove him into a breakdown and St. Patrick's hospital. Recalling it in the Poe-induced dream, he can comment on it in critical terms, blaming the whole unnatural catastrophe on the rigorous strictures of the Catholic Church: "O could the Church have allowed us pessary, thin cover, / I would not so abuse what others coveted" ('Pilgrimage', *CP,* 358). So Poe's women are a displacing code for "Margaret." And by locating him in sexual sites, giving a focus to his imagination for what could not be achieved in "life", Poe's work propelled Clarke inadvertently towards becoming the poet he grew into after the "Margaret" affair, a poet acutely aware of the gap between desire and mundane facts, aware of the originating power of blocked erotic energy. In the hidden but essential parts of himself, that is, both Poe and Whitman offered Clarke a reality he had, no matter in how curbed or distorted a way, to get into his own work. Often this reality pushes against the more voluntary and deliberately accommodated influences of the Revival, and has to wait until the later poetry for more direct expression.

Poe, Longfellow, and Whitman, then, seem to have left distinct marks on what lies under and before Clarke's growth as a poet; on his nervous sense of rhythm, his sexual identity and distress, the anger that leads to satiric vitality and personal reticence. In addition, and much later in his career as a poet, there is Pound. Beginning in repugnance, Clarke's recorded attitude to Pound describes an arc of increasing approval, rising from his 1940's description of the *Cantos* as "a gigantic poetic notebook in which [Pound] has jotted down, with a minimum of rearrangement and simple parallelism, everything that strikes his fancy in the midst of his extensive reading".[26] What Clarke objects to here is a lack of formal order, the apparent disorder of Pound's method naturally disturbing a poet who is himself (see *Night and Morning*, 1938) obsessive about tight closed forms posited upon principles of metaphysical and aesthetic selection and willed limitation.

By 1950, however, a more benevolent note creeps in. Now Pound's "ragbag of the centuries" is "a gigantic patchwork quilt to keep young poets warm".[27] Finally, by 1960, after Clarke's own re-emergence as a poet with a renewed relationship to the whole notion of form, he can seem almost envious of Pound's openness, of "his poetical forms ... so ample in their freedom that they seem devoid of technical controls".[28] At the same time he was ready, predictably enough, to praise Pound's "energy and zeal", his "quarrel with his own country".[29] And Pound's surrender to plenitude may arguably have had some impact on the latest work of Clarke, in some of which ('Old Fashioned Pilgrimage' itself, for example) the expansive manners of Pound and Whitman may have been drawn into the circle of Clarke's own laden expression.

On the speculative side, too, though one would not want to push this too far, it's possible to detect connections between those acts of creative *translation* performed by Clarke as well as Pound. This could be true of Clarke's late adaptation of Ovid ('The Dilemma of Iphis'), which is reminiscent in voice of some of Pound's great translations. It might also be true of some of those much earlier translations by Clarke, his adaptations and re-animations of the Irish (in *Cattledrive in Connaught,* and in *Pilgrimage),* where the Irish poet seems to perform something of the same service for Celtic and Medieval Ireland as Pound (in *Personae,* 1908-1910) did for Provençal and Medieval Italian literature. Like Pound, Clarke both brings the old works into a recognisably modem idiom, and at the same time "translates" some of his own experiences into the poetic idiom of the earlier culture. Without direct evidence, of course, this has to remain a possibly interesting parallel of literary achievements, a farther, if speculative link between the Irish and the American poet. All in all, however, these acquaintances suggest that in the grain of Clarke's poetic achievement there is a definite American presence, both in the deeper layers of the imagination and in the more distinctly tangible areas of form.

Nothing suggests an early American influence on Padraic Fallon. Some critical views, however, as well as a number of poems of his maturity show that Fallon used Ezra Pound to help him cast off the obviously heavy (and disturbing) burden of Yeats. What he takes from Pound seems at once formal and substantive. His praise for Pound's "loosening verse line" and open form, for example, is posited on the ability of such formal instruments to accommodate all aspects of the individual in a way that is not available to the "careful stanzas" of Yeats.[30] Pound offers Fallon encouragement for his own emerging, aesthetic bent towards a "free-for-all [of] personal language".[31] Stimulated by American practice, he argues against the English Auden's rationale for closed forms, and he sounds like a Black Mountaineer with an Irish accent when he declares that the poem should make "its own rules of rhythm and pattern ... personal to the poet".[32] There's a remarkably prescient and refreshing quality to Fallon's further critical remark that "each poem is different from any other and demands its own kind of language and approach".[33]

This aesthetic pragmatism (which makes Fallon sound more like the contemporary of Montague and Kinsella than their elder by a generation) was enriched even more in 1957 by the Irish poet's discovery of William Carlos Williams. In this case, the American influence prompted arguments for a poetry of "normal human range," free from the larger gestures of Yeatsian magniloquence, since "The big tower," as he says in one poem, "would have us / Make our verse like his, sing / Jubilant Muses".[34] The effects of such critical and theoretical views are most in evidence in the agile relaxed fluencies of such poems as 'The Head', 'For Paddy Mac', or 'Painting of My Father' ("So you wanted little of me towards the end, / Barbering, a light / For the old pipe, / And an ear, my ear, any ear, when you spilled over / The intolerable burden / Of being a very old man"). The particular influence of Pound may be detected especially in 'Stop on the Road to Ballylee'. In this poem, recording a journey to honour Yeats's centenary, Fallon can be seen, ironically, embracing the poetic legacy of Pound in the poem's patchwork as it moves between the voice of the mind, a Latin text, and the external spectacle of patients in the grounds of an asylum. The subject matter itself has to be an oblique declaration of the reason why such a formal stretching is necessary—otherwise how encompass a world of such daunting variety, a world that will not lend itself to neater formulations, no matter how masterful their rhetoric.[35] Poems like these underline the serious ways in which Padraic Fallon (a poet whose true value and importance have still not been properly recognised) serves as a conduit for the American presence in contemporary Irish poetry.

Denis Devlin is the most deliberately cosmopolitan of the poets in the generation immediately after Yeats. Although it is the European influence that's usually cited in this regard (Valéry in particular),[36] the American influence, which helped him become "one of the pioneers of the international poetic English which now prevails on both sides of the Atlantic" (as his American commentators said of him),[37] is impossible to overlook. His collegial friendship with American poets such as Tate, Warren, and Ransom had to foster such an influence, which seems also to have been a way (as was his use of the Europeans) to avoid the difficult shadow of Yeats. The American pressure on the work may be felt in a comparison between the first and second volumes of Devlin's verse. The following stanza is from *Intercessions (1937)*:

> Me seeing the seen, the prestige of death drives faint,
> Coupled asynchronous like time and knowledge.
> Lunar scaffolding, a decrepit star falls,
> Rotting eyelashes fall through fetid wind.
>
>   ('In the Last Resort')

It is a task to unravel the stiff, hermetic obscurities of these lines. Linguistically muscle-bound, their rhythmic push is nervously staccato, far from speech. The poems in the next book, however, *(Lough Derg*, 1946) are "more accessible in their increasing ease both in line and language", qualities which may be attributed to a specifically American influence—to Tate, Warren, maybe Stevens, Hart Crane.[38] Here is how 'Ank'hor Vat', a poem in that volume, begins:

> The antlered forests
> Move down to the sea.
> Here the dung-filled jungle pauses.
> Buddha has covered the walls of the great temple
> With the vegetative speed of his imagery.

It is easy to see how the clotted syntax, turgid abstractions and claustrophobic lines of the earlier mode have given way to a colloquial yet dignified ease, an expression quick and unencumbered, moving in varied lines along the edge of direct 'prose' statement. This "Americanisation" of Devlin's work (a shift which heightened, I believe, the native drift and ability of his imagination) is even more apparent in 'Annapolis', where direct speech and relaxed narrative manner remind of Frank O'Hara. This is how it begins:

> 'No we can't get a license for liquor, being too near the church,'
> Said the waiter. The church looked friends enough
> On its humble grassy hillock. So I said: 'Excuse me
> I must have a drink.' And I rambled on down West Street
> To eat and drink at Socrates the Greek's.

Finally, the American presence in Devlin's work can be confirmed by the "Projective" openness of the later 'Memoirs of a Turcoman Diplomat', with its echoes of Pound's Mauberly, or of some of Stevens's dandyish effects, a touch of Ransom's sly, spry pedantry:

> Tuck in your trews, Johannes my boy, be led by me,
> These girls are kind. And we're all the rage now,
>   whiskey-flushed men of our age,
> The callow and the sallow and the fallow wiped off the page.

It is influences like these that nourish Devlin's own various, sophisticated voice and chameleon manner—his eclectic, thoughtful, idiosyncratic habits of imagination which left their mark on poets like Montague and Kinsella. By such distinct means he helps to blaze a path away from Yeats—who in terms of a certain sort of influence could be a dead end for an Irish poet—a path marked out at least in part by the Americans.

Oddly enough, perhaps, it is Patrick Kavanagh, poet of the parochial, who is most vocal in that generation about his debts to American poetry. For this reason one has to take with the usual spoon of salt (necessary accompaniment to a great many of Kavanagh's *ex cathedra* critical pronouncements) the poet's response to the question, "What do you think of modern American literature?" The answer was a single shot from the hip: "Trash."[39] The truth of the matter is that Kavanagh drank deep at this Transatlantic well, and was the first Irish poet to bring American influence into its post "modernist" phase, post Pound and Eliot, that is. As for the other poets mentioned, for him too this influence seems to be one way out of the Yeatsian cul-de-sac.

Kavanagh's submission to American influence falls into two phases. The first brings him into contact with the Imagists and

Gertrude Stein. The lucid, hard-edged quality of the Imagists "excited my clay heavy mind," he says, while Stein's "work was like whiskey to me, her strange rhythms broke up the cliché formulation of my thought."[40] Both in the Imagists and in Stein he found the encouragement to be "hard and clear," undecorative, to *present* image and "to make full use of free verse."[41] He admired the work of J.G. Fletcher, most likely valuing its ability to be emotional in a direct, unsentimental way.[42] The fact that Imagism "praises by showing" edges the influence out of the formal and into the area of feeling, of a particular attitude to the subject.[43]

Basically, then, Kavanagh first went to technical and emotional school to the Americans, learning what he could from the poets in Conrad Aiken's anthology, *Twentieth Century American Poetry*. By 1947 he is knowledgeable enough to say that for him the best American poets are "Dickinson among the women, after Millay, a sentimentalist [not necessarily, as Kavanagh uses the term, pejorative], and among the men some very good such as Frost, Wallace Stevens, E.A. Robinson, Jeffers, John Peale Bishop, Hart Crane, Richard Eberhart, and young Harry Brown, a new poet influenced by Yeats. All these men are perhaps in the Main Stream."[44] Thanks to this tutorial in American poetry, Kavanagh could move from the brief stanzaic structures of his first book to the larger visionary reach and suppler technical accomplishment of *The Great Hunger*. Here's a stanza from an early lyric, 'A Star':

> Beauty was that
> Far vanished flame,
> Call it a star
> Wanting better name.

It's easy to hear the gap between that sort of thing and lines like the following from *The Great Hunger*—with their more casual formalities, their sense of spoken language, their quick shifts of perspective:

> Maguire knelt beside a pillar where he could spit
> Without being seen. He turned an old prayer round:

'Jesus, Mary and Joseph pray for us
Now and at the hour.' Heaven dazzled death.
'Wonder should I cross-plough that turnip-ground?'

Kavanagh's second phase under the influence of American poetry departs from the Main Stream, connecting up with the overflowing tributary generated by the Beat poets. This coincides more or less with his own poetical "re-birth" in the mid-50s. He sees their work as an antidote to what he objects to in the "artificial verbalism" of Richard Wilbur and others, and his attitude to them in 1958 is part mockery, part envy: "That rascal Allen Ginsberg has made news with the beat generation ... You only have to roar and use bad language. I am genuinely thinking of having a go."[45] Later he says he still likes "the fun and games of a lot of contemporary verse ... even people like Ginsberg to some extent, funny stuff."[46] It is the vitality he admires: Ferlinghetti, he says, is 'alive' (as opposed to 'very dead' Robert Lowell).[47]

What Kavanagh gets from the Beats is the encouragement to exercise his own talent in a *relaxed* way—beyond lyrical posture and beyond even the great colloquial performance of *The Great Hunger*—for "they have all written direct, personal statements, nothing involved, no, just statements of their position. That's all."[48] It was this sort of encouragement which led him to the "direct, personal statements" of such later poems as the Canal sonnets, 'Is', 'The Hospital', and 'Auditors In': here even rhyme is relaxed statement:

> I am so glad
> To come accidentally upon
> Myself at the end of a tortuous road
> And have learned with surprise that God
> Unworshipped withers to the Futile One.

The Americans, then, marshaled Kavanagh the way that he was going, along a path that was deliberately (and for later Irish poets most helpfully) charted away from the more rhetorically imposing figure of Yeats. Nourished by the Americans, Kavanagh found a poetic voice that did not falsify his powerful sense of the actual or betray his conviction that "what is called art is merely life". That his American schooling was of central importance to him as a poet is sadly confined by the fact that, when he runs dry at the end, even "an American anthology" can grant him no inspiring jolt:

> I have perused an American anthology for stimulation
> But the result is not as encouraging as it used
> To be when Walter Lowenfels' falling down words
> Like ladders excited me to chance my arm
> With nouns and verbs.
>
> ('In Blinking Blankness')

The strongest and most lasting effect of the random, often haphazard, usually occasional uses of American influence by these four important poets in the generation after Yeats (that the Northerners MacNeice and Hewitt seem untouched by this influence is a fact that may at some point be worth following up, as another indicator of differences between poetry written out of distinct historical and cultural traditions [and conditions] in the island), is to aid in the establishment of a fresh base for Irish poetry in the modem world for which Yeats felt such contempt. American poetry, that is, helps steer Irish poetry in a direction quite distinct from that pointed to by Yeats's last wilful testament and exhortation in 'Under Ben Bulben'. Whether the Americans are "base-born products of base beds" or not, it's clear that these Irish poets do not "scorn" them (and we remember that Yeats himself began with one radically modem American as teacher, and proceeded to the school of another). Rather do the Irish poets make their own uses of certain Americans on a journey that moves away from Yeats and towards their own identities as poets of contemporary Ireland and the contemporary world. In one way or another, Clarke, Kavanagh, Devlin, and Fallon lay the ground between them for two major poets of the next poetic generation— John Montague and Thomas Kinsella (Richard Murphy's apparent freedom from that influence might, of necessity, be part of the discussion that would include MacNeice and Hewitt)—to flower fully within the sphere of American influence. Taking for granted the working of this particular influence in their immediate predecessors, impelled, both by their reading of these predecessors and by their own experience, towards the Americans, they have richly re-discovered this influence for themselves and incorporated it organically into their work.

Both Kinsella and Montague deepen and extend the American influence in a conscious effort to become truly modem Irish poets. The American influence also helps them break from their first influences—French poetry in Montague's case, Yeats and Auden for Kinsella. More than their predecessors, these two have made American poetry a distinct, articulate part of their own development as poets. Even in personal terms the two seem emblematic of new conditions in this literary relationship: Montague was born in America, and later literally "went to school" (at Yale, Iowa, Berkeley) to American poets. Kinsella—between 1965 and the late '80s—lived part of every year in America.[49]

"Ireland," Montague has said, somewhat mischievously, "is an island off the coast of Europe, facing across three thousand miles of water towards America."[50] Aside from having spent his first six or so years there, he spent some poetically formative years, 1953-56, attending Yale, Iowa, and living on the West Coast. Given his respect for Pound, Eliot, Stevens, Williams, and Crane ("probably the best generation of poets since the Great Romantics"),[51] it was natural for him to turn to America. Ransom, at Yale, he says, was "instrumental in changing my destiny",[52] Williams once "hugged me like a son"; Snodgrass, Bly and others were at Iowa with him; Lowell and Wilbur were known on the East Coast, and Ginsberg and Snyder on the West: meeting them, "I seemed to have completed the spectrum of my own generation of American poetry."[53] Williams helped him towards a "low-pitched style [that] seeks exactness," ("Waiting," in *A Chosen Light),* while in the work of Robert Duncan he was encouraged in a natural tendency of his own—a habit of touching the ordinary with ritual grace, a glimmer of myth. It was also most likely Duncan who tuned him to the depths of possibility in the term "political poetry".[54]

From early on, Montague saw the American influence as a necessary complement to the Irish: "I am not saying that Ezra Pound is necessarily more important than Egan O'Rahilly for an Irish poet (one has to study both) but the complexity and pain of the *Pisan Cantos* are certainly more relevant than another version of 'Preab San Ól'.[55] Both content and form in American poetry helped Montague realise his own poetic identity, learning from that "complexity and pain" of Pound and from the "new music" which Pound and Williams brought into English verse, prompting the realisation that the iambic line was no longer able to register "the curve of modern speech".[56] In form and language, as well as content, American poetry has helped Montague become what he calls "a global regionalist," a poetic citizen of the world.[57] And at a deeper level, it helps him do greater justice to his own doubled, or tripled, identity—Ulster-Irish-American. It may be, indeed, that the American influence / presence / nourishment helped Montague deal with the ambiguities inherent in such a layered identity, helping him distance himself creatively (i.e. with no loss of feeling) from the intimate intensities of his personal, communal, or political subject matter. In addition, by crossing Lowell with Snyder, Creeley, Ginsberg and Duncan, he imports into Irish poetry a rich array of poetic resources for dealing with the autobiographical. In writing about the self he has learned to be lyrical and detached, a combination not as truly available to him in the expansive sonorities of Yeats nor in the much more relaxed but often rawly personal exposures of Kavanagh (who as a lyric poet remains much more *vulnerable* than Montague ever seems to be).

The result of Montague's reception of the Americans may be seen in the following stanzas. First, these lines from an early poem:

> A rainy quiet evening, with leaves that hang
> Like squares of silk from dripping branches.
> An avenue of laurel, and the guttering cry
> Of a robin that balances a moment,
> Starts and is gone
> Upon some furtive errand of its own.
> ('Irish Street Scene With Lovers', 1952)

In this descriptive "scene", external texture is what matters, as it does in the rest of the poem. The self is nowhere, all is external, adjectival. Even the title accentuates the analogy with painting. On the other hand, the opening stanza of Montague's quintessential Sixties (in Ireland) poem—the poem that, maybe more than any other, registered a waking up, "The Siege of Mullingar"—suggests something of the way his style relaxed under American influences:

> At the Fleadh Cheóil in Mullingar
> There were two sounds, the breaking
> Of glass, and the background pulse
> Of music. Young girls roamed
> The streets with eager faces,
> Pushing for men. Bottles in
> Hand, they rowed out a song:
> *Puritan Ireland's dead and gone*
> *A myth of O'Connor and Ó Faoláin.*

There's a distinct new sound here, something that goes beyond description and enters the realm of action. Rhythmically it is very relaxed, yet there's a tension in the phrasing itself, as in those young girls "pushing for men." The plain diction has a ritual edge to it (pulse, roamed, the breaking), culminating in the elegiac, slightly comic refrain that deconstructs Yeats and "September 1913." In this pliancy of expression, lyrical narrative has taken over from description, enhancing the deliberately un-iambic movement towards an easy, elegant, but decisively un Yeatsian balancing of stanza and sentence. The openness the poet seems to be celebrating is inherent in his own formal management as well as in the life freshly surging around him. So Montague's encounter with Irish matter in idioms that live under the influence of American poetry helps him to his own voice, his own poetic identity, free not only of the Revival, but of Kavanagh too, as in the following lines from a later poem:

A slight fragrance revives:
cycling through the evening
to a dance in Gowna—Lake
of the Calf, source of Erne—
with one of the Caffreys.
Our carbide lamps wobbled
along the summer hedges, a
warm scent of hay and clover
as, after the dance, I kissed
my girl against a crumbling
churchyard wall.

('A Slight Fragrance', *The Dead Kingdom*)

Here the brief lines bolster the mythic allusion with ordinariness, as Montague shows Williams' or Synder's feel for effective brevity. A narrative bone keeps lyrical description honest, while the run of the lines, gathering towards a sentence, prohibits any iambic dependence. This is the Kavanagh of 'Inniskeen Road' salted with a rack of American suggestions. This is Montague's own possession of the "new music" he has mentioned.

Which brings me back to that most idiosyncratic of contemporary poetic musicians, Thomas Kinsella. From the start, says Kinsella, "the things behind form were what bothered me, having to do with content, exploratory form—the sequence rather than the finished single object... longer, sequential forms, open-ended—so that the effort can continue inside a more stable continuum."[58] Like Yeats with Pound, Kinsella managed to remake himself under the influence of, again, Pound, then Williams and, most likely, Lowell. In adhering to the "wonderfully enabling free forms" of the Americans, Kinsella felt he was turning to the center of modern poetry in English.[59] For, as he says in 1966, "at some point [during the last twenty-five years], the growth point of contemporary poetry shifted from England to America."[60] The Americans helped him proceed beyond the influence of Yeats and the influential "grace" of Auden, to "find much more satisfaction in the form of Ezra Pound's *Cantos*. Finally I don't think graceful postures are adequate; you have to deal with the raw material."[61]

Dealing with the "raw material," the Americans liberated him into a "dynamic response to whatever happens".[62] Like Yeats, who was a profound example in this respect, these American poets encouraged Kinsella to think of the *totality* of a poetic career, as they helped Montague towards his commitment to the poetic *sequence.*

Probably the most important lesson Kinsella learned from Williams was to bring form and content together in especially fertile, fructifying ways. This was "a kind of creative relaxation in the face of complex reality; to remain open, prehensile; not rigidly committed."[63] In a poetry where "commitment" is difficult to avoid (Yeats's stratagem was to be absolute, serially, for different things; very little about his magniloquent stanzaic adventures suggests "creative relaxation"), Williams's kinetic scepticism offered a way out to Kinsella, a Keatsian lesson translated into American. Creative agility, imaginative openness: in the substantive and formal consequences of such terms, Kinsella is the Irish poet who has most internalised them. These American lessons sanction to Kinsella's own mind the continuous, open-ended nature of this enterprise. And, seen in this light, his work (as well as that of Montague) owes much (aside from the *Cantos)* to such American examples as *Paterson, Notebooks, History,* the *Maximus* poems, *Howl, Kaddish, Dream Songs,* and of course to the granddaddy of them all, *Leaves of Grass.* Such American sequences taught both these Irish poets how to forge a language and a form adequate to the particular span and nature of their personal and public experience. And taught them, too, how to be implicitly more "political," in the broadest meaning of that word.

In its development and change, Kinsella's work is most exemplary of the way the American presence can affect Irish poetry. (Even more than Montague, he discovered and made use of it after his own early style was firmly established.) The following brief passages—the first from 'Mirror in February' (1962), the second from 'Worker in Mirror, At His Bench' (1973)—may serve to illustrate this.

Below my window the awakening trees,
Hacked clean for better bearing, stand defaced,
Suffering their brute necessities,
And how should the flesh not quail that span for span
Is mutilated more? In slow distaste
I fold my towel with what grace I can,
Not young and not renewable, but man.

What may be heard first in this passage is the iambic insistence of the line, the deliberate sense of closure, the firm architectural snap as it shuts on that conclusive foot. Abstractions are obvious, too, "brute necessities" being both spare and eloquent (if a bit self-consciously *gestured),* as is the slightly posed syntax of the rhetorical question. The emblematic account of the landscape is also worth noting: the poet reads the surroundings in a way that goes back to "That time of year thou May'st in me behold" and beyond. It is a given trope, brilliantly handled. The nature of the experience, therefore, is being clearly seen from the outside, and in all this Kinsella is the masterful manager of given conventions, of what he himself calls "received forms and rhyme".[64]

In what sounds like his own version of some of the tenets of Projective Verse, Kinsella describes his later poems as "[having] a form which ought to be felt as a whole, rather than in, e.g., stanzaic expectations. Each poem has a unique shape, contents and development".[65] The impulse, he says, is "merely to understand, not to impose order".[66] Where 'Mirror in February' seeks "to impose order," I'd say 'Worker in Mirror, at His Bench' reflects the impulse "merely to understand," trying to show something like Williams's "creative relaxation in the face of complex reality."

It is tedious, yes.
The process is elaborate, and wasteful
—a dangerous litter of lacerating pieces collects. Let my rubbish stand witness...
Smile, stirring it idly with a shoe.
Take, for example, this work in hand:
out of its waste matter

it should emerge light and solid.
One idea, grown with the thing itself,
should drive it searching inward
with a sort of life, due to the mirror effect.
Often, the more I simplify,
the more a few simplicities go
burrowing into their own depths,
until the guardian structure is aroused...

Most satisfying, yes.
Another kind of vigour, I agree
—unhappy until its actions are more convulsed: the 'passionate'—
might find it maddening.

In this passage Kinsella is committed to no climactic truth, but
to a "dynamic response to whatever happens" (rather than "the
music of what happens"). Here every thing is interiorised, the
mind's voice seems much closer to its source than in the earlier
poem. Matching this, the iambic line has been broken into a line
that's more responsive to phrase/sense units, and to units of breath.
Rhyme is gone, lyrical diction is gone, and syntax is fractured and
hesitant, articulating the way the mind itself proceeds.
Consciousness here turns into speech, with almost no
intermediaries, and reflects upon itself, not upon some world
external to it. We're less aware of the thing made than of the
making itself, as tones shift and unspoken nuances slide between
one utterance and the next. Metaphor seems not at all imposed,
but found in the language itself as a direct response to perception
(as in "guardian," "waste matter," "aroused"). There is no sense of
a finished architecture, an architecture of finish, of conclusions. All
is process, and this is confirmed by the ending of the poem, which
is simply an unfinished period ("from zenith to pit / through
dead"). Consciousness is speaking here, not being spoken about. I
might even hazard that it is the American revolution in his own
verse that enables Kinsella to get beyond the poetic influences of
Yeats and Auden to the prose virtues of articulated consciousness
that Joyce offers in *Ulysses*. If for Stephen Dedalus the shortest way
to Tara is via Holyhead, the shortest way to a native Irish

consciousness in modem poetry may be via Paterson, New Jersey, and Hailey, Idaho.

After the deliberate attachment of Kinsella and Montague to poetry written by Americans, it's been easier for Irish poets to take American influence as a natural feature of their own verse. So the enlargement of Seamus Heaney's style by the benevolent presences of Frost, Lowell, or Elizabeth Bishop—his accommodation within the borders of his own disciplined habits of what he calls "the drift of contemporary American verse"[67]—doesn't come as a surprise. In moral as well as technical terms, too, Lowell's has been as instructive a career to Heaney as the starker model of Mandelstam, while in books like *Station Island, The Haw Lantern,* and *Seeing Things,* the American habit of sequence-making has left its mark. Derek Mahon's best work, too, with its sceptical ironies and plangent lyrical intelligence may carry some signs of Lowell, Hart Crane, Richard Wilbur and Elizabeth Bishop. And in the remarkable poems of Paul Durcan, I think most of us would hear a voice that betrays something of the emancipated energy of the Beat poets—part bardic, part comic-strip, part spiritual effervescence.[68] In a more incidental way, Ciaran Carson has acknowledged that the spell-binding narrative strategies of his recent poems are indebted to the long fluent line of the American poet C.K. Williams. And even the rapt enigmatic manners of Medbh McGuckian may, or so the critics say, owe something to Hart Crane (and, I would add, to Emily Dickinson and Marianne Moore).

While showing an increasingly American presence in Irish poetry, these more recent individual connections do not signal any radical innovations or significant new departures. In the work of Eavan Boland and Paul Muldoon, however, the American influence has—as it has at other pivotal moments over the past hundred years—brought important new elements into Irish verse.

Feeling herself orphaned in her own predominantly male native tradition, Eavan Boland found in the American tradition a powerful and persistent female presence. In that remaking of herself that entailed turning away from her earliest lyric manner,

Boland seems to have drawn in particular on two poets—Sylvia Plath and Adrienne Rich. First—to fashion a more recognisably female voice speaking specifically female truths—it is to Plath she turns, to the Plath of reckless self-exposure, of nervous extremities vehemently controlled by compressed lines and closed-circuit stanzas. The Plath you can hear in this snatch of 'Medusa':

> Green as eunuchs, your wishes
> Hiss at my sins.
> Off, off, eely tentacles!
>
> There is nothing between us.

In *In Her Own Image* Boland adapts this voice to her own uses, to chart some general truths about the female condition and to speak about the female body and a woman's relationship to it in a novel, often bitter, but unflinching way. Her 'Tirade to the Mimic Muse' sets the purgative tone:

> I've caught you out. You slut. you fat trout.
> So here you are fumed in candle-stink.
> Its yellow balm exhumes you for the glass.
> How you arch and pout in it!
> How you poach your face in it!

Writing such "rhythms of struggle, need, will, and female energy", Boland amplifies her range in *Night Feed*, drawing this time on some of the quieter, more domestic tones and cadences of Plath. In the later poems of *The Journey* and *Outside History*, however, she moves out of earshot of Plath and into range of Adrienne Rich. Rich's politicising of women's territory has also fed Boland's critical stances, while the Irish woman's choice of a public role as poet has in part been enabled by the American's exemplary career. Rich's poetic language is much less hectic than Plath's, and this has led, I'd imagine, to the more quietly accented speech of Boland's recent poems. Certainly this later work seems like a tuned response to Rich's own self-instruction in that splendid feminist allegory of hers, "Diving into the Wreck": "I have to learn alone / to turn my body without force / in the deep element."

Boland's work—tutored by her chosen American connections—has helped younger Irish poets who happen to be women find their voices and their courage. In this it has altered the map of Irish poetry. That map isn't so much altered as re-invented by the startling work of Paul Muldoon. And it almost goes without saying, that in this first thoroughly postmodern imagination in Irish poetry the American presence is palpable from the start. Muldoon's ludic mode co-opts a whole rack of American presences to his own purposes. The eclectic early narrative, 'Immram', for example, splices an old Irish voyage tale to tough guy detective stories in the manner of Raymond Chandler:

> She was wearing what looked like a dead fox
> Over a low-cut sequined gown,
> And went by the name of Susan, or Suzanne.
> A girl who would never pass out of fashion
> So long as there's an 'if' in California.

Likewise, 'The More a Man Has, the More a Man Wants' grafts onto a dark tale of violence in the mean streets of the North of Ireland some elements from native North American trickster stories. And Muldoon's latest opus *Madoc, A Mystery,* narrates in his own mysterious and mischievous way an hallucinatory encounter between Europe (more specifically the British Isles) and the New World. This is only a sample, but it's enough to show how deeply America is implicated in Muldoon's work, so deeply as to make specific debts to specific poets a moot point. He himself has said that "it's important to most societies to have the notion of something out there to which we belong, that our home is somewhere else." His own discovery of America as one such "out there" has turned that "somewhere else" into a home, into a brave new world of possibilities that enable him to deal—in ways as compelling as they are oblique—with some of the most pressing political issues of his own native Northern Ireland.

Because the eclectic collage excitements of America have illuminated Muldoon's work from the start and in such a seemingly natural and undogmatic way, he represents a logical conclusion to this story. His work, indeed, may be taken as emblematic of the speed with which one can now move between Ireland and America. Times Square, after all, is not too many flying hours from Harold's Cross. But in the hundred years or so since Yeats sat in that house in Harold's Cross, thinking of Walt Whitman and a school of Irish poetry, the poetry of Times Square (or Harvard Square or San Francisco Bay) has been a consistently nourishing source to which Irish poets have turned and by which they have been replenished. Although it hasn't been the only influence, what we now know as modem Irish poetry in English would be very different without it.

But why has this been the case? In the modem and contemporary poetry of Great Britain, after all—leaving aside Auden, Thom Gunn, and some recent poetry by women—no such deep and extended connection with America seems to exist. It's probably not possible to answer with any completeness that question. But in the story as I've told it, two common threads seem to have run through the examples. Yeats, remember, was influenced by Whitman in what we might call ideological ways and by Pound in more explicitly aesthetic/stylistic ways. Likewise, in all the other cases I've mentioned, stylistic and "ideological" elements seem closely bound. For, in all of them, American influence seems synonymous with freedom—whether freedom from a colonial condition, freedom from socio-cultural or racial clichés, freedom from a powerful predecessor, freedom from a confining state and state of mind into a mode of freshly expressive consciousness, freedom from that confinement caused by the politics of gender, or freedom from any and all the easy labelings of cultural, political, and poetical rhetorics. Since to treat properly the implications of this fact would need another essay, I'll simply end with a fairly rudimentary formulation of "stylistic" and "ideological" factors that have played their part in this game of influences. The formulation combines two descriptive statements. The first is John Montague's revisionist description of Ireland's geographical location: "Ireland," said Montague, "is an island off the coast of Europe facing across three thousand miles of water towards America". The second statement belongs to Thomas Kinsella, who in 1966 observed that "at some point in the last 25 years, the growth point of contemporary poetry shifted from England to America". What I deduce from these two statements—taking them lightly enough and yet seeing some subversive nerve twitching under each of them—is that the variously inflected American connection I've been describing is merely a logical part of the continuing (perhaps now completed) effort at achieving the comprehensive autonomy of Irish poetry in the English language.

'The American Connection', was first published in *Facing the Music: Irish Poetry in the Twentieth Century* (Crieghton University Press, USA, 1999); thanks to Creighton University Press for permission to reprint the essay here. An earlier, shorter version entitled 'American Relations' was included in *Irish Poetry Since Kavanagh* (ed. Theo Dorgan, Four Courts Press, 1996).

NOTES

1 Thomas Kinsella, *Davis, Mangan, and Ferguson? Tradition and the Irish Writer,* (Dublin: Dolmen Press, 1970) 57.

2 James Randall, Interview with Seamus Heaney, *Ploughshares.* 5. 3. (1979) 20.

3 W.B. Yeats, *Collected Letters,* eds. John Kelly and E. Domville, vol. I (London: Oxford University Press, 1986) 9.

4 *Letters, 339.*

5 *Ibid,* 408, 409.

6 In "A New Poet" (review of poems by Edwin Ellis). See *Uncollected Prose of W.B. Yeats,* ed. John Frayne, vol. I (New York: Columbia University Press, 1970-1976) 234.

7 "Dr. Todhunter's Irish Poems" (review, 1892, of *The Banshee and Other Poems),* in Frayne, 216.

8 "Song of Myself," *Leaves of Grass* (New York: Penguin Books, 1982) 42,73.

9 W.B. Yeats, *Essays and Introductions* (New York: Macmillan, 1961) 521.

10 "Upon a House Shaken By the Land Agitation," *Poems* (1951) 93.

11 "Of an evening in Woburn Buildings, it is reported that [Douglas] Goldring thought that Pound had succeeded in reducing *Yeats* from master to disciple." Frank Tuohy, *Yeats*

(London: Macmillan, 1976) 47.

12 A.N. Jeffares, *W.B. Yeats, Man and Poet* (London: Routledge & Kegan Paul; New Haven: Yale University Press, 1949) 176-77.

13 Ezra Pound, "The Later Yeats," in *Literary Essays of Ezra Pound* (New York: New Directions, 1968) 379.

14 Letter to Lady Gregory, December 10,1909, in Allen Wade (ed). *The Letters of W.B. Yeats* (London: Rupert Hart-Davis, 1954) 543.

15 *Ibid.*

16 Tuohy, 147.

17 *Modern Poetry* (London: Oxford University Press, 1938) 71. MacNiece says that Whitman "Is all for affirming everything, he forgets to negate" (72), and he claims that Whitman's poetry demonstrates "'democracy' in the worst sense" (72).

18 *Ibid, 164.*

19 *Ibid, 186.*

20 *Ibid, 18.*

21 *Ibid, 203.*

22 *Twice Round the Black Church* (London: Routledge and Kegan Paul, 1962) 162. 23 *Collected Poems* (Dublin: Dolmen Press, 1974) 358-59.

24 *Ibid.*

25 See, for example, *Mnemosyne Lay in Dust* in *Collected Poems,* 336, and *A Penny in the Clouds* (London: Routledge and Kegan Paul, 1968) 44. Also see Part II of "The Death of Cuchullin" in the first edition of *The Sword of the West* (Dublin: Maunsel and Roberts, 1921) 53-59. Clarke excluded this from the revised version in *Collected Poems.*

26 G. Craig Tapping, *Austin Clarke: A Study of His Writings* (Dublin: Academy Press, 1981) 229.

27 *Ibid,* 230. The quotations here are from reviews for *The Irish Times.* See Tapping's Appendix for full list.

28 *Ibid.*

29 *Ibid.*

30 *The Bell,* 17. 8 (1951) 59.

31 *Ibid,* 17. II (1952) 53.

32 *Ibid.*

33 *Ibid, 54.*

34 "Stop on the Road to Ballylee." *Poems* (Dublin: Dolmen Press, 1974) 61.

35 Given the voice and general manner of this poem, it may even be possible to see its locale as a covert allusion to Pound in St. Elizabeth's. But no external evidence 1 know of supports such a speculation.

36 See Denis Devlin, *Selected Poems,* edited by Allen Tate and Robert Penn Warren (New York: Holt, Rinehart and Wilson, 1963), Introduction, 13.

37 *Ibid,* 14. The work of Devlin's friend and contemporary, Brian Coffey (19051995), should also be mentioned, whose "Missouri Sequence" (1962) and *The Death of Hektor* (1979) show the influence of Pound and Eliot.

38 John Montague, "The Impact of International Modem Poetry on Irish Writing," in *Irish Poets in English: The Thomas Davis Lectures on Anglo-Irish Poetry,* ed. Sean Lucy (Cork and Dublin: Mercier Press, 1973) 149-50. Both Montague and Kinsella have always insisted on the importance of Devlin's example to their own broadening of poetic horizons.

39 *November Haggard: Uncollected Prose and Verse of Patrick Kavanagh,* ed. Peter Kavanagh (New York: Peter Kavanagh Hand Press, 1971) 96.

40 *The Green Fool* (London: Penguin Books, 1975) 244. He adds, "it was in the American poets I was chiefly interested."

41 Pound's Imagist Manifesto, cited in John Nemo, *Patrick Kavanagh* (Boston: Twayne, 1979) 40-41. See also 38-41.

42 See *Lapped Furrows: Correspondence 1933-1967 Between Patrick and Peter Kavanagh,* ed. Peter Kavanagh (New York: The Peter Kavanagh Hand Press, 1969) III. Kavanagh raises this and subsequent points in advice to his brother about a series of lectures on modem poetry, in August 1947.

43 *Ibid.*

44 *Ibid,* 113. The oddest omission from his list is William Carlos Williams, since Kavanagh, in a sense, ended up doing for Irish poetry what Williams did for American—bringing poetry home to ordinary life in an authentically ordinary language with a capacity for genuine lyrical lift-off.

45 *Ibid, 219.*

46 *November Haggard,* 91 (from an interview in May, 1964).

47 *Tri-Quarterly,* 4 (1966) 109. In a symposium "Poetry Since Yeats: An Exchange of Views," at Northwestern University, which broke up in disorder with Kavanagh arguing against Kinsella (and everybody else) over the particular merits of contemporary poetry. This might be an emblematic moment in the history of American influence on modem Irish poetry.

48 *Ibid, 110-111.*

49 Before this, only Devlin had had any practical exposure, being Irish Consul in New York from 1939 to 1947.

50 "The Impact of International Modem Poetry on Irish Writing," in Lucy, 144.

51 *The Literary Review,* 22 (1979) 173.

52 "John Montague: An Interview," *Verse* (Oxford) 6 (1986) 35.

53 *TLR,* 22 (1979) 157.

54 This is an assumption I am making, knowing Montague's admiration for Duncan (See *TLR* above, 157-58 and in Lucy, 157), and Duncan's profound ability to fuse political and personal issues.

55 In Lucy, 153.

56 *Ibid, 156.*

57 Title of interview in *TLR.*

58 *Viewpoints, 104.*

59 *Ibid,* 106.

60 *Tri-Quarterly,* 4 (1996) 105.

61 *Viewpoints,* 104.

62 *Ibid,* 108. *63 Ibid,* 106. *64 Ibid,* 108. *65 Ibid,* 109. *66 Ibid.*

67 *Ploughshares* 5.3. (1979) 19. He has also had his political/poetical consciousness tuned by these West Coast encounters.

68 The poems of James Liddy, who has lived for many years in America, reveal similar influences, while their gay sexuality also connects them with distinct strains of recent American verse, as can be seen in "The Voice of America 1961", in which he addresses "Daddy Whitman".

"That Blank Mouth":
Secrecy, Shibboleths, and Silence
in Northern Irish Poetry

DAVID WHEATLEY

The poetry of contemporary Northern Ireland has been among the most highly praised and widely read of any in English since the emergence in the 1960s of the generation of writers that includes Seamus Heaney, Michael Longley, and Derek Mahon. All are complex, allusive poets who have achieved popular readerships despite the presence in their work of much that resists being easily understood by readers who stand outside their poetry's densely local, mythic, and, on occasion, private references. This aspect of their style is particularly evident in the work of writers such as John Montague, Heaney, Paul Muldoon, and Ciaran Carson, whose roots lie as much in the Gaelic as in the English-language tradition. Writing on the proliferation of "cloaked references to Gaelic culture or Irish history" in modern Irish writing in English, Dillon Johnston identifies "two kinds of unstated or suppressed references":

> first, those omissions introduced to frustrate a colonial auditor
> and convey secrets to a primary audience, and, second, those
> omissions introduced into a song or story when the fuller

context is lost over time or simply dropped because in a place
as small as Ireland everyone knows the plot.[1]

Johnston contrasts this secretiveness with English models such
as Wordsworth's preface to *Lyrical Ballads*, with its commitment to
a pellucid colloquial register, and Philip Larkin's aversion to poems
decked out in the arcana of what he disparagingly calls the "myth-
kitty." Possible roots for this cultural opposition can be found,
Johnston reminds us, in Counter Reformation habits of secrecy or
equivocation, conferring poems with the metaphorical equivalents
of "priests' holes [and] secret rooms" in which to conceal their
deeper meanings.[2] In a contemporary context, these habits take on
new resonances as historical themes and memories combine with
the self-consciously Modernist techniques of Heaney's place-name
poems or Carson's fantastical cityscapes of Belfast in the Troubles.
In these poems, secrecy and indirection become both subject and
means, as the poet attempts to satisfy the impulse to flee the
brutality of a violently divided society, while simultaneously
realizing that there is no escape and that the signs and symbols of
division are coded into the most apparently innocuous subjects. All
language teems with dangerous possibility, needing the corrective
example of silence to keep it in its place; 'Whatever You Say Say
Nothing,' Heaney famously instructs himself in the title of a poem
from the second section of *North*. The value of silence is
trumpeted, even as the silence is breached in the selfsame act. In
'The Stone Verdict,' for instance, we read of the poet's recently
dead taciturn father:

> It will be no justice if the sentence is blabbed out.
> He will expect more than words in the ultimate court
> He relied on through a lifetime's speechlessness.[3]

In commemoration of the dead man, "Somebody will break [the
silence] at last to say, 'Here/ His spirit lingers,' and will have said
too much" (Heaney, p. 17). In repeating the speaker's lapse into
speech, Heaney pointedly flouts the code of manly silence which

he professes. The poem, that is to say, calculatedly tropes rather than literally upholds its suspicion of speech. In many different ways, Heaney and other Northern Irish poets deploy strategies of silence, secrecy, private reference, and tribal shibboleth rather than "blabb[ing] out."

Although these strategies may superficially appear to work against self-expression, in reality they can yield up unsuspected layers of meaning in the most unusual ways. The precedents for this in Irish literary tradition are as frequently comic as they are elegiac or tragic. Confronted with a section devoted to the Irish language in *The Best of Myles,* a miscellany of the Ulster novelist Flann O'Brien *aka* Myles na gCopaleen's columns for *The Irish Times,* non-Gaelic-speaking readers may be tempted to move along swiftly to the next chapter. As an admission of defeat, this would be somewhat premature, since, on closer inspection it emerges that many of these Gaelic columns are not quite as inhospitable as they appear. An illustration to one passage hints at colonial confrontation of some kind. An official-looking type is scrutinizing a document at a table while a group of soldiers searches the room; the dejected bystanders, we assume, form the subjects of this military attention. The characters are given names from Irish folksong, such as Sheán O Duibhir a' Ghleanna and Eamon a' Chnuic. Some of their conversation is in Irish, but most is, in fact, in English, transliterated into Gaelic orthography. The tableau ends with the rebels confronted with the evidence of their sedition:

> Shean O Duibhir: Namh deintilmein díos documaints ár bhearigh sióruigheas, iú hav nó reispeict for ló and óirdiur—
> Fear na mná ruaidhe: God séabh dé Cbhín.
> Sheán O Duibhir: iu sbheign;
> Sheán Buidhe: Aigheam glad tú saoí dat bhun obh iú ios loigheal. Reilís thim and loch de odars up, só dat de me leirn tú bí gúid and loigheal suibdeicts obh thur mós gréisius maidistigh. Díos tú ár a disgréis tú thur aighrís suibdeicts.[4]
> [Sheán O Duibhir: Now gentleman these documents are very serious, you have no respect for law and order—
> Fear na mmá ruaidhe: God save the Queen.
> Sheán O Duibhir: you swine;

Sheán Buidhe: I'm glad to see that one of you is loyal. Release
him and lock the others up, so that they may learn to be good
and loyal subjects of her most gracious majesty.
These two are a disgrace to her Irish subjects.]

As a mini-drama of Irish problems with language and the law,
this recalls a celebrated passage in James Joyce's early journalism.
Writing for a Triestine newspaper, *Il Piccolo della Sera*, in 1907,
Joyce described the case of another Myles/ Miles: his near
namesake Miles Joyce, an Irish-speaking peasant from the West of
Ireland on trial for murder in an English-speaking court. The
figure of this dumbfounded old man," he wrote, "a remnant of a
civilization not ours, deaf and dumb before his judge, is a symbol
of the Irish nation at the bar of public opinion."⁵ What for Joyce
was emblematic of tragic cultural alienation, in Myles na
gCopaleen's hands has become latter for scholarly farce. The divide
between English, the language of imperial law and order, and Irish,
the language of secrecy and treason, is blurred in a ridiculous
hybrid. Neither one extreme or the other, this nonsense language
illustrates a failure of communication, but one that produces
surplus rather than a lack of signification, for those who can crack
the Milesian code. "All great poetry is written in dialect," Craig
Raine has written, with Dr. Johnson's description of Milton's
language as "Babylonish dialect" in mind. "It follows," he goes on,
"that [...]it is all poised between sense and non-sense."⁶ Joyce and
Myles na gCopaleen are just two examples of the long historical
precedents in Irish writing for this dialectal no man's land between
sense and non-sense, silence and incomprehension: *"Hirp! Hirp!
for their Missed Understanding! chirps the Ballat of Perce-Oreille,"* as
Joyce puts it in *Finnegans Wake*,⁷ a work before whose exacting
tribunal it is the fate of many readers to stand deaf and dumb.

While strategies of evasion, codes, shibboleths and other
language games are now standard postmodern fare, there are
obvious reasons beyond the literary *Zeitgeist* why these devices
come into particularly sharp focus in contemporary writing from
Northern Ireland. In the past three decades and more, the Troubles

have provided an inevitable and tragic backdrop, warping their social deformations into the fabric of Northern Irish writing. Challenged by events that defy representation, from the mid-1960s onwards Northern Irish poets and playwrights have made of language itself a site of contestation. Comparing Andrew Marvell to Heaney, Longley, Mahon, and Muldoon in an influential essay, Christopher Ricks wrote of the artistic implications for a society rent by civil war: "first, an intense self-reflexive concern with the art of poetry itself in poems; and second, a thrilled perturbation at philosophical problems of perception and imagination," contributing to the prevalence of what he terms the "self-inwoven simile" in these writers' work.[8] Superficially, images of non-communication would appear to point towards un- rather than inweaving of poetic detail, but as the example from Myles na gCopaleen shows, there are many ways in which communication fails to fail so totally that something, however bizarre or unexpected, does not get through. Silence itself may be unchanging, but in the words of another connoisseur of non-communication, Samuel Beckett's *Malone*, "The forms are many in which the unchanging seeks relief from its formlessness."[9] Among the forms of this formlessness which demand examination are the works of Friel, Heaney, and Muldoon, and especially, the poetry of Ciaran Carson.

The classic example of dramatically exploited linguistic confusion in recent Irish theatre is Brian Friel's *Translations*, about the impact of the Ordnance Survey, whose job it is to render all Gaelic place names into English, on the Irish-speaking community of Baile Beag in Donegal. In a simple but brilliant dramatic coup, all Irish-language dialogue in the play is given in English, although it remains incomprehensible to the non-Irish-speaking Royal Engineers. This allows Friel to make the non-communication of culturally alien groups dramatically viable; it should be pointed out, however, that just as Irish is silently elided into English, the dichotomy of these alien groups also results from a strategic elision, since Friel has chosen to ignore the roots of the Ordnance Survey in Irish antiquarianism, the better to present it as a blunt instrument of colonial administration.[10] In one passage of multi-layered irony, the young woman Maire pronounces a sentence in English ("In Norfolk we besport ourselves around the maypoll" [sic]),[11] in a "strange" accent because of her difficulties with the language that she (or rather, the actor playing her) is of course already speaking. At times this device leads Friel into straightforward absurdities, as when Doalty "derives" the word "conjugation" from the Latin *conjugo* (*Translations*, p. 25), a plausible enough result until one remembers that the Irish word for conjugation is not derived from and sounds nothing like this Latin root. By making Irish so all-important and yet invisible at the same time Friel strengthens the association that he makes between language and a condition of almost mystic inwardness. When the guardsman Yolland becomes infatuated with Donegal culture and tries to learn Irish, he is forced to recognize his lack of entitlement, whatever his linguistic skills:

> Even if I did speak Irish I'd always be an outsider here, wouldn't I? I may learn the password but the language of the tribe will always elude me, won't it? The private core will always be ... hermetic, won't it? (*Translations*, p. 40)

For the first half of the play, these cultural misunder-standings are more humorous than anything else, but in the one passage in which the Irish language is used, the colonial difference reasserts itself in implacable and irreducible form. Yolland has gone missing, and fearing the work of local malcontents, Captain Lancey announces a series of measures to be taken unless he returns, ending with the leveling of all houses in a list of townlands, he reads in English, with Owen translating. Threatened with being wiped off the map, in every sense, the original place-names become tokens of impotent authenticity, signifying only themselves in the harsh new dispensation. Immediately afterwards, Lancey begins to question Sarah, who has a speech defect, asking her name. The terrified girl symbolically "closes her mouth" (*Translations*, p. 62), the combination of political menace, language barrier, and speech defect erecting a powerful obstacle in the way of communication.

Mention of place names and language inevitably calls Seamus Heaney to mind. His classic statements on this theme are the toponymical poems of *Wintering Out* such as 'Anahorish,' whose place name shades into the place itself, with its "soft gradient/ of consonant, vowel-meadow," and 'Toome,' which begins with the poet again taking vocal possession ("My mouth holds round/ the soft blastings,/ Toome, Toome.")[12] The scale of commentary that these poems have provoked is in striking disproportion to their slender dimensions, to the point where they have become as fought over as the place-names they trope. W.J. McCormack states the case against perhaps the best-known example of all, 'Broagh,' the townland whose rhubarb-blades "ended almost / suddenly, like the last / *gh* the strangers found / difficult to manage" *(Wintering Out,* p. 27):

> place is presented as an oral achievement in these poems, the enunciation of sounds which are infinitely refined, unique, beyond the ability of "the strangers" whose attempts to manage the specific consonant they had visited are nicely cast in the perfect tense, "found." In these last lines some occupation, some mastery by strangers has been resisted (if not repulsed) by the language/landscape.[13]

While there is undoubtedly a substantial component of linguistic nostalgia in 'Broagh,' to see the mastery of the place-name as a surrogate for the repossession of the territory from the same "strangers"—and thus a covert piece of nationalist pugnacity—would be to oversimplify. As has been noticed by favorable and hostile critics alike, despite the Gaelic origin of the place name in *bruach,* meaning "riverbank," nowhere in the poem does Heaney limit the mastery of its difficult gh sound to Protestant or Catholic.[14] Further, the poem contains many words ("rigs," "docken," "boortrees"), which, although also difficult for the stranger, are of Ulster Scots, not Gaelic origin.[15] And lastly, despite the British army's being the most obvious candidates for the "strangers" of the penultimate line, there is strictly nothing to stop the phrase's applying to passing French or German tourists, unfriendly as this may seem. The poem is thus both excluding and, in a strange way, reconciliatory; although judging the poem "based on a convenient fiction," Neil Corcoran finds 'Broagh' a "celebration of exclusiveness, we might say, in the interests of local inclusiveness" *(The Poetry of Seamus Heaney,* pp. 45-46). The unifying vocable presages in microcosm a culture unified enough for the term "strangers" no longer to carry overtones of sectarian division. Nevertheless, and for all these subtleties, the fact remains that 'Broagh' identifies this utopian hope with a localized speech-act or shibboleth, failure to master which carries severe consequences and ultimately exclusion from its imagined community. Heaney's younger contemporaries are far less confident about drawing such equivalences between local belonging and poetry's utopian content.

A poem such as this exemplifies the sort of fastidious and, to an outsider, perhaps exasperating preoccupation with local detail that Philip Larkin has in mind in 'The Importance of Elsewhere' when he speaks of "The salt rebuff of speech,/ Insisting so on difference," although Larkin goes on to speak of this very quality being what "made me welcome": "Once that was recognised, we were in touch."[16] Heaney refuses to extend so easy a welcome, questioning the universality of pastoral conventions and preparing the way for the assault on his own easy-going, youthful pastoral style that will come in his fourth book, *North* (1975). Part of the reason for his withholding assent from a universally inclusive language, except as a function of a utopian future, is Heaney's knowledge of the baleful power of what Yolland called "the language of the tribe." The prose poem 'England's Difficulty,' published at the same time as *North,* offers an example of this tribal language in its title, coming as it does from the slogan "England's difficulty is Ireland's opportunity." The speaker says of himself:

> An adept at banter, I crossed the lines with carefully enunciated passwords, manned every speech with checkpoints and reported back to nobody. [17]

Instead of rejecting the coerciveness of the checkpoint interrogation, familiar from poems such as 'The Frontier of Writing,' Heaney internalizes it and applies it to his own speech. By reporting "back to nobody," he underlines the gratuitousness of his behavior, but also its secretiveness, the acquired watchfulness of his speech.

Another striking example of this, again from *Wintering Out*, is the poem 'Bye-Child.' Here, according to his author's note, Heaney writes about an idiot child "discovered in the henhouse where [his mother] had confined him. He was incapable of saying anything." But as with Sarah in *Translations*, his silence is reconfigured as a form of eloquence in its own right:

> But now you speak at last
>
> With a remote mime
> Of something beyond patience,
> Your gaping wordless proof
> Of lunar distances
> Travelled beyond love.
> (*Wintering Out*, p. 72)

The child's silence is exemplary of his innocent patience and undemonstrative love, but these qualities are crucially beholden to the poet, through whose agency they "speak at last." The impediment of dumbness is accorded its dignity, but only from the controlling position of the fully capable speaker. The question of poet as spokesman is crucial to *North*, in which Heaney alternately exults in and interrogates his role as poetic sponsor for the silent bodies recovered from the bog. It is the poet of 'Bye-Child,' however, whom we must to keep in mind and contrast with the more disturbing strategies of Muldoon and Carson.

The work of Paul Muldoon has long been a point of comparison for readers of Heaney; in a recent essay, Neil Corcoran has argued that the two men's work forms the most important interrelationship (personal and intertextual) of any among Northern Irish poets.[18] But as Corcoran shows, it is a relationship driven (on Muldoon's side) by scepticism as well as admiration, ranging from mild joshing to outright slander (the implicit characterization of Heaney as Southey in *Madoc* springs to mind). If Muldoon's readings of Heaney appear in his work in coded form, they do so in keeping with the spirit of private jokes, coded utterance, and secrecy that animates so much of Muldoon's poetry. The title of one of his most celebrated volumes, *Quoof*, is itself a secret, "a family word for hot water bottle" which Muldoon carries to bed with him as he sleeps with a woman in New York, who in any case speaks "hardly any English."[19] Published as it was in the aftermath of the Republican hunger strikes of 1981, *Quoof* puts its interest in secrecy to frequent use in the volume's many poems on political themes. One such exemplary poem is the elliptic quatrain 'Mink':

> A mink escaped from a mink-farm
> in South Armagh
> is led to the grave of Robert Nairac
> by the fur-lined hood of his anorak.
> *(Quoof,* p. 28)

Captain Robert Nairac was one of the most notorious British undercover agents in Northern Ireland, a Grenadier Guardsman who worked as a liaison officer for the SAS and RUC [20] in South Armagh, traditionally the most fearsome of Republican strongholds; he also figures in Michael Longley's 'On Slieve Gullion.' Before its escape the mink's body had been due for industrial processing, just as according to legend Nairac's body was disposed of in a meat processing plant, his body never having been found after his abduction and murder. The unknown whereabouts of a grave bear emotive resonances in Irish politics: the location of

Robert Emmet's grave is famously unknown, while more recently attempts have been made to locate the graves of abducted and disappeared Irish Republican Army victims. Commenting on the mink sniffing out Nairac's grave by "the fur-lined hood of his anorak," Tom Herron has written of "the futile attempt to find partnership, to establish connections."[21] Where Heaney's metaphors in 'Broagh' are utopian and connective, freely conjoining the language and landscape, Muldoon's metonymy is grimly dissociative with only an anorak standing in for the corpse, which, in any case, holds no interest for the mink who finds it.

As an undercover agent moving between communities, Nairac has much in common with the slippery Gallogly and Mangas Jones of 'The More a Man Has the More a Man Wants,' the long poem with which *Quoof* ends. Carrying out intelligence work in the Republican community Nairac was famously reckless in his attempts at disguise, dressing in cowboy uniform and speaking in a Belfast accent beneath which his Ampleforth, Oxford, and Sandhurst background was all too obvious.[22] One result of his close contact with the Catholic community was his strategy document, 'Talking to People in South Armagh.' In it Nairac stresses the need for sensitivity to the shibboleths involved in addressing the locals: "Never ever use the words INFORM, INFORMATION, WITNESS or INTIMIDATE. Never write anything down; it smacks of police work. Never offer money for INFORMATION." The aversion to writing is an almost parodic embrace of oral culture by a representative of the intelligence-gathering security forces, but it is part of the general drift in Nairac's remarks away from a model of brute domination to a more subtle hegemony, based on verbal cajoling and manipulation. In a list of 'Useful Euphemisms,' he outlines some of the ways in which the cultural divide can be obscured in mannerly small-talk: rather than "Can you give me any information?" the agent should say, "Perhaps you might be able to help" for "The Provos are stupid murderers," "Some of the boys have gone too far"; and for "Your son is a terrorist," "Your son is taking up with a bad crowd."[23] The watchwords for the successful agent should be tact and cunning understatement, qualities Nairac himself so singularly failed to display. Nevertheless, his warning against using the word "inform" showed a sound instinctive grasp of Irish history. As James Joyce, a writer for whom betrayal amounted to a controlling obsession, wrote in his early article 'Il Fenianismo,' "In Ireland, at the proper moment, an informer always appears" *(Critical Writings,* p. 189).

For Muldoon, all language is shadowed by the threat of betrayal, against which it defensively encodes itself in forms such as the cryptic 'Mink.' In the case of *Madoc,* an entire volume is presented as a massive rebus, while in 'Capercaillies' from the same book he smuggles a cheeky acrostic about a well-known American magazine down the left-hand margin. The more recent collections, *The Annals of Chile* and *Hay,* explore audacious rhyme schemes, with poems rhyming between one book and another, onomastic puns, excavated etymologies, and other flamboyant writerly signatures. Frequently, Muldoon introduces an extra dimension of self-reflexivity by troping on the production of sound itself, and treacherous sound at that. In 'Third Epistle to Timothy,' from *Hay,* Muldoon once again demonstrates the process by which sectarian difference is graphed onto and in turn read back from language. The poet's father has hired himself out as a servant boy on a Protestant farm, where he is treated as a figure of suspicion:

> "Though you speak, young Muldoon ..." Cummins calls
> up from trimming the skirt
> of the haycock, "though you speak with the tongue
> of an angel, I see you for what you are ... Malevolent.
> Not only a member of the church malignant but a
> malevolent spirit."[24]

Later on, Muldoon describes the kidnapping by Republicans of an octogenarian county grand master of the Orange order, the improbably named Anketell Moutray,[25] an act which turns the poet's thoughts to Land League affrays and other agrarian unrest, culminating in another image of literally linguistic violence:

> It shall be revealed ...
> A year since they cut out the clapper of a collabor ... a collabor ...
> a collaborator from Maguiresbridge. *(Hay,* p. 100)

As we heard from Captain Nairac, no one is more steeped in infamy in Irish history than the informer, perhaps explaining Muldoon's stuttering unwillingness to pronounce the word "collaborator," allowing as it does for a near-homonym on "clapper" in the same line, not to mention *clabaire*, Irish for clapper and also meaning "an open-mouthed person." The collaborator's mouth is open only so that its tongue may be cut out.[26]

But more even than Muldoon, it is the Belfast-born Ciaran Carson who has explored the poetry of secrecy and shibboleths. Like Flann O'Brien, Ciaran Carson was raised in an Irish-speaking household, learning English only when he went to school. After a promising first collection in 1976, *The New Estate and Other Poems,* he observed a creative silence of over a decade before re-emerging with the universally lauded *The Irish for No* in 1987. The collection's title carries an echo of "Ulster Says No," the slogan of Unionist resistance to the Anglo-Irish Agreement of 1985, as well as providing Carson with a foolproof exemption from the binaries of Ulster politics: there is no Irish for no, or yes either, for that matter. Thus, it is not just the Paisleyite slogan that fails to translate, as Carson shows by debating with his companion on how to render into Irish the slogan of the Ulster Bank, "the Bank that Likes to Say Yes": *"The Bank That Answers All Your Questions,* maybe?"[27] Carson's Belfast is, to borrow Roland Barthes's phrase for Japan, an empire of signs, and one possessed of all the inscrutability of orientalist cliché. 'Snowball' begins with the words "All the signs," before listing the paraphernalia of 1960s femininity ("beehive hair-do, white handbag, lettos, split skirt") *(Irish for No).* The woman disappears to an unknown destination past the loading bay of "Tomb Street GPO," on what the poet guesses is a blind date, but like her fishnet "everything is full of holes." The holes in the poem's continuity are temporal as well as spatial: next day the poet awakes to a postcard inviting him to "Meet me usual place & time tomorrow", but dated 9 August 1910. As Corcoran has written, the "card in a hole in a Tomb" is a very dead letter indeed."[28] Carson's father worked as a postman, and in 'Ambition' we read that his jokey franking of a letter with the harp on the back of an Irish ha'penny led to his never being promoted: more important matters than dead letters fall through the net of circulating signifiers that is Belfast's empire of signs.

The inscrutably arbitrary sign returns in 'Calvin Klein's Obsession,' which goes in search of the past by way of its associated tastes and scents. An opening taste of beer reminds the poet of the Ulster Brewery, which reminds him of the perfume Blue Grass and the fur worn by an old girlfriend. The glorious insubstantiality of the woman from the past could not be further from the exhumed female figures of *North*. What he felt for the girl, "infatuation," "Was a vogue word," hinting at the magazine in which these various perfumes are advertised and heightening the sense of artificiality so that "it wasn't all quite real." Later, he wonders of the Blue Grass fragrance, "How often did she wear it anyway?" and "can it still be bought?" The blurring of experience is heightened by a (not quite accurate) quotation from Edward Thomas' 'Old Man': "I sniff and sniff again, and try to think of what it is I am remembering."[29] Earlier in that poem Thomas puzzles over the disjunction between name and object: the essence of the herb "Old Man, or Lad's-love" "clings not to the name," but as he adds, "And yet I like the names." What makes Carson's woman so wraithlike is also what keeps his feelings so strong, inhabiting as she does a condition of pure anonymity: "For there are memories that have no name." The memories proceed through buying snuff for his grandmother to, by association, a list of perfumes from the 1930s and 1940s, until in the final lines, the poet remembers his childhood habit of wearing his mother's high heels and breathing in the "flesh-coloured dust" of her powder compact. *"Or maybe it's the name you buy, and not the thing itself,"* the poem wistfully concludes *(Irish for No, p. 25).*

In 'Belfast Confetti,' a poem that shares its title with his next collection, Carson makes the chaos of violence scriptable in metaphors drawn from writing and printing, but in ways that emphasize its explosive effects on any pretence of realist representation: as the riot squad move in "it was exclamation marks,/ ... a fount of broken type," while an explosion makes "an asterisk on the map." The poem ends with what sound like existential questions ("What is/ [m]y name? Where am I coming from? Where am I going?"), but which in the context are almost certainly the barked enquiries of a policeman, "A fusillade of question-marks" *(Irish for No,* p. 31).

Military intelligence, surveillance, and codes play a ubiquitous role in Carson's work; when, as often happens, *Belfast Confetti* registers some difficulty in communication it is as though the work is experiencing a form of technical interference or static. Maps feature frequently, too, and typify this representational difficulty: the prefatory poem 'Turn Again' describes maps with an excess of information ("a map of the city which shows the bridge that was never built/ A map which shows the bridge that collapsed; the streets that never existed") and maps that are covered in blanks ("the shape of the jails cannot be shown for security reasons.")[30] Rather than brand them inadequate to the absent reality, Carson insists on the fluid nature of the city itself, in the Borgesian formulation "[t]he city is a map of the city" *(Belfast Confetti,* p. 69). In 'Serial,' Carson says of a hotel in the border county of Fermanagh that

> since the Ormsby
> Room in Lakeland still remains un-named, they are thinking of
>   calling it
> Something else: not a name, but the name of a place.
> *(Irish for No,* p. 51)

How can the room be unnamed, we wonder, if Carson tells us its name. The prospect of giving somewhere "not a name, but the name of a place" is reminiscent of the White Knight's distinctions between his song, the name of his song, and what the name of his song is called in *Through the Looking Glass.*[31] There may be a private joke here on the name of Carson's poet contemporary Frank Ormsby; equally, in what is a running joke in Carson's work, a reference to Carson is not to the poet himself but, of course, to his namesake Edward, the bellicose and fanatical founder of modern Unionism.

It is not just what they represent that makes maps and writing suspect; the very materiality of their inscriptions too shows signs of untrustworthiness. In 'Queen's Gambit,' we read of the "frottage effect":

> the paper that you're scribbling on is grained
> And blackened, till the pencil-lead snaps off, in a valley
> of the broken alphabet.
> *(Belfast Confetti,* p. 35) [32]

Even the most functional forms of writing fall short: the *T* and *r* of a shop called Terminus are missing in 'Gate,' leaving the school grade-like message *"e minus,"* appropriately enough, as the failed shop is advertising a closing-down sale *(Belfast Confetti,* p. 45). A tea-stained copy of *The Irish News* in 'Queen's Gambit' blurs the text to the point where the paper is "difficult to pick up without the whole thing coming apart in your hands" (p. 38), not unlike the devices of which the poem speaks elsewhere. Speech too is only intermittently susceptible of representation. While two winos can "converse in snarls and giggles, and . . . understand each other perfectly" *(Irish for No,* p. 40), where more is at stake, the system of codes and secrecy asserts itself more strongly. Someone whispering into an answer phone does so as into a confessional box, giving secret details of "names, dates, places" *(Belfast Confetti,* p. 37). Soldiers enter a chemist shop and seem to "spit word-bubbles" at the assistant, but

> Much of this is unintelligible, blotted out by stars and
> asterisks
> Just as the street outside is splattered with bits of corrugated
> iron and confetti.
> *(Belfast Confetti,* p. 33)

The confetti here, as in the title, refers to the "conveniently hand-sized" *(Belfast Confetti,* p. 12) half-bricks and other detritus used by rioters for lobbing at the security forces. If Belfast's red-brick façades are synonymous with Victorian industry and respectability, these half-bricks confirm their altogether different associations with their alternative labels *"heeker"* and *"hicker."* The confetti image here suggests street violence through linguistic defamiliarization, but in 'Jump Leads' Carson powerfully suggests a far more violent scene by apparently returning the word to its more familiar sense. The poem describes a news report of a murder:

> Everything went dark. The killers escaped in a red Fiesta
>   according to sources.
> Talking, said the Bishop, is better than killing. Just before
>   the Weather
> The victim is his wedding photograph. He's been spattered
>   with confetti.
> *(Belfast Confetti,* p. 56)

The journalese of "according to sources" and the Bishop's pious enjoinder exist within the bland continuum of reportage that allocates the murder victim a minute or two before moving on o the weather, although not before we have seen him in a wedding photograph. In a stark reduction, the victim "is" his photograph; the coldness of this contrasts with the sociability of the occasion recorded, a wedding, at which the victim has been "spattered with confetti." Imprisoned in ts repackaging for the news camera, the celebratory confetti has become unmistakably deadly in meaning, just as in 'All the Better to See You With' it forms part of a dark retelling of the Little Red Riding Hood story. Later, in 'Queen's Gambit', the poet is listening to a barber talk about a Republican operation, uncomfortable that he may have been mistaken from his short hair for an ex-prisoner. The mirror he looks into is used by Carson to mirror his unease, although here too images go aslant:

> And I've this problem, talking to a man whose mouth is a
>   reflection.

I tend to think the words will come out backwards, so I'm
saying nothing
(Belfast Confetti, p. 39).[33]

Other examples of Carson's defamiliarizing technique appear just as he seems to extend the 'reassuring hand of cliché: "I know this place like the back of my hand," he tells us in 'Question Time' *(Belfast Confetti,* p. 57); but in 'Bloody Hand' he has already reminded us that the Red Hand of Ulster originates in an act of mythic self-mutilation, "hacked off at the wrist and thrown to the shores of Ulster" *(Belfast Confetti,* p. 51). And as he says in 'Question Time,' "who really knows how many hairs there are, how many freckles?" on the back of a hand, repeating his scrutiny of the same cliché in the earlier poem '33333.'

'The Mouth' again shows Carson dispersing a violent subtext beneath superficially harmless clichés: "There was this head had this mouth he kept shooting off" *(Belfast Confetti,* p. 70). When matters deteriorate for the overly loquacious mouth, "provisionally," it has become inevitable that "[b]y the time he is found there'll be nothing much left to tell who he was." Heaney's articulation of his identity on behalf of the dumb boy in 'Bye-Child' looks like an act of benevolent sponsorship; here identification at second-hand has become gorily forensic, a piecing together of dismembered body parts whose powers of expression have been viciously extinguished.[34]

Puzzling over the etymology of Belfast in the prose poem 'Farset,' Carson has recourse to the Irish-English dictionary of Father Dineen, who offers a generous array of meanings for the word *fearsad:* "a shaft; a spindle; the ulna of the arm; a club; the spindle of an axle; a bar or bank of sand at low water; a deep narrow channel on a strand at low tide; a pit or pool of water; a verse; a poem" *(Belfast Confetti,* p. 48). Taking the last of these meanings, Carson suggests a translation for Belfast as "mouth of the poem; for which he derives an extra sanction from the fact that one of the other meanings of *fearsad,* a "turn in the furrow," is a secondary meaning of the Latin *versus (Belfast Confetti,* p. 49).

Readers of Muldoon's Clarendon lectures, *To Ireland, I,* will recognize the tone of straight-faced jiggery-pokery behind these fanciful etymologies, but Carson is not the first writer to notice Father Dineen's madcap polysemousness. Myles na gCopaleen offers the example of a sentence that could be translated uncontroversially as "It is entirely a new thing that a symphony concert should be held in conjunction with a Gaelic choir"; when put through the Dineen mill it comes out as "It is longitudinally a strong anxiety that a wise and vigorous ancient Irish ale should be in moderato time at once with an unsophisticated troop" (Best of Myles, pp. 277-78).[35] Where a return to etymological roots in Friel or Heaney offers the chance of digging down to solid and authenticated ground, in Carson's hands it has become akin to opening a never-ending series of trapdoors under the fabric of his poems. Standing in for a language whose speakers, like Flynn in the poem 'Dresden,' can call on thirteen words for a cow in heat, Carson's "second language" is no less zany, nor the linguistic maps he draws up in it any more reliable.

One of the final poems in *Belfast Confetti,* and one of Carson's most powerful, is 'John Ruskin in Belfast.' Although not picked up on by Carson, 'Revised Version' earlier in the book offers a possible reason for Ruskin's attraction to the city, with its allusion to George Macartney, "Sovereign of Belfast in the late 1600s," who described the city as a "second Venice" *(Belfast Confetti,* p. 67). Carson cites 'The Mystery of Life and Its Arts,' a pastiche Ruskin text in which the critic ascribes Irish neglect of "[e]xternal laws of right" to their "strange agony of desire for justice; their tormented national character blocking their ability to pursue aesthetic excellence. For (Carson's) Ruskin, the religious art of Old Irish missals is childlike and artificial, while an angel he describes is tellingly, or rather untellingly, short of a crucial detail:

> See how in the static mode of ancient Irish art, the missal-painter
>   draws his angel
> With no sense of failure, as a child might draw an angel, putting
>   red dots

In the palm of each hand, while the eyes—the eyes are perfect circles, and,
I regret to say, the mouth is left out altogether.

Carson comments:

> That blank mouth, like the memory of a disappointed smile,
>   comes back to haunt me.
> That calm terror, closed against the smog and murk of Belfast:
>   Let it not open
> That it might condemn me. Let it remain inviolate.
> *(Belfast Confetti,* pp. 97-98)

Unlike Heaney in 'Bye-Child,' Carson makes no attempt to act as intermediary for the silent figure, choosing instead to honor its "inviolate" silence. This is not an act of trans-historical solidarity such as we find in the poems about silenced figures from the past by Carson's contemporary, Eavan Boland; Carson fears that if the angel did speak, it would be to condemn him. He refuses to flatter us with artificial claims for his ability to bridge the divides of history; nor will he turn this failure into forms of self-castigation in which the guilty poet (as so often in Heaney and Boland) is placed center-stage.

If the title of Carson's 1993 collection, *First Language*, suggests a Heaneyesque at-homeness in his idiom, the inclusion of a preliminary poem in Irish reminds us that what follows is, in the title of the volume's second poem, in Carson's 'Second Language.'[36] John Goodby has argued that this and Carson's more recent work represent "a brave move beyond the communal and local material of the earlier collections to an investigation of the principles which underlay them,"[37] a shift reflected in the "hieroglyphic alphabet," "Typewriterspeak" and "general boggledybotch" of their new style, to use the book's own self-description.[38] What *First Language* has in common with *Opera et Cetera* (1996), is Carson's application of his semiotic method not just to his stock themes of traditional music, military intelligence, and the urban labyrinth, but more and more, and more self-consciously too, to the surface of language itself. The first of the four sequence that make up *Opera et Cetera*, 'Letters from the Alphabet,' extrapolates from Rimbaud's great sonnet 'Voyelles,' with its synaesthesic character sketches of the five vowels. Working through all twenty-six letters, Carson allows the abecedary accidents (to give an example of my own) of the English language to guide the course of his poems. Thus, 'A' is about a Stealth bomber whose Alpha wing carries an Ampere-wired Ampoule-bomb.[39] For the eighth letter of the alphabet, Carson begins with an incident about a change of contractor for the provision of sausage rolls to the prisoners in Long Kesh, Belfast's notorious H-shaped prisons. The prisoners complain, but trivial-sounding as the incident is,

> We cannot reproduce his actual
>   words here, since their spokesman is alleged
> To be a sub-commander of a movement deemed to be illegal.
> (*Opera et Cetera*, p. 18) [40]

Under the terms of broadcasting legislation, it is the prisoner's voice that is unacceptable, whether he uses it to talk about politics or the size of prison sausages; by lip-synching his words, the phonocentrically superstitious authorities prevent him generating his own oxygen of publicity. Outside the prison, it is again the nature and grain of the voice heard on the news rather than what it says that attracts attention. Carson draws on the fact that the aspirate/non-aspirate pronunciation of the letter *h* functions as a sectarian marker in Northern Ireland, in a way the broadcasters have evidently mistaken:

> His "Belfast" accent wasn't West enough. Is the H in H-Block
>   *aitch* or *haitch*?
> Does it matter? *What we have we hold? Our day will come?*
>   Give or take an inch.
>
> Well, give an inch and someone takes an effing mile. Every
>   thing is in the ways

You say them. Like, the prison that we call Long Kesh is to
the Powers-that-Be *The Maze.*
(*Opera et Cetera,* p. 18) [41]

The difference between opposing tribal shibboleths ("What we
have we told," "Our day will come") is insignificant, or no more
significant than the inch which Carson considers giving or taking.
Even the mile that will follow from unwisely giving the inch,
however, is an alphabetic quibble, an "effing" mile, just as the
powers are powers that "Be," all lost in the "Maze" of their
confusions. The second sequence, 'Et Cetera,' continues Carson's
assault on monoglot verse by assigning familiar Latin tags as titles
to each section. The third, a set of translations from Romanian, is
suitably titled 'Alibi,' while the last, 'Opera,' is based on radio
operators' code, which spells out another alphabet from 'Alpha' to
'Zulu.' This final poem recapitulates the verbal self-inweaving that
is now the dominant note in Carson's work. Beginning by
imagining himself as a Zulu soldier, he dances round soldiers like
"a hound of Baskerville" *(Opera et Cetera,* p. 92). A description of
his soldier foes as "typecast phalanxes" hints irresistibly at
Baskerville type and the fictive nature of the battles that Carson
fights "foraging behind the alphabetic frontier," in "the gargled
doggerel of this dumb poet." The reference to his dumbness is a
reminder that, unusually or not for this celebrant of the oral
tradition, Carson has a pronounced stutter, in reaction to which he
exults in the silent freedom of reading and writing, as in this poem.
Hence the description of his speech, when he does talk, as "garbled
doggerel," compounded by the play with codes, shibboleths, and
silence which even as a child, Carson learns to view as allies rather
enemies of what he wants to say.

In Captain Nairac's terms, his is a poetry that may "witness" but
never "informs," in all the ambiguity of the latter term. Like
Muldoon, Carson is a writer forever "insisting so on difference," to
the point of misunderstanding and even incomprehensibility.
Rather than obscurantism on his part, however, this refusal to treat
his medium as one of transparent limpidity is richly productive

rather than preventive of poetic effect. Carson's stance is not unlike the angel at the end of 'John Ruskin in Belfast,' from the "sealed tomb" of whose mouth come the words *"Be thou there / Until I bring thee word."* The angel's words to the Holy Family are a source of comfort amid the Massacre of the Innocents that the poem describes, even if what they say is only that the angel will speak again some time in the future rather than anything more immediately reassuring. The mix of supernatural comfort and impotence is a perfect emblem for the relationship to his tragic subject matter that characterizes Carson's poetry. Speaking, or rather not speaking for a whole tradition in Irish writing that places silence at the heart of its understanding of speech and poetry, Carson's angel could be relied on to satisfy the dead man of Heaney's 'The Stone Verdict': when his blank mouth finally opens to speak, we can be sure that whatever he says, it will not have been "too much." As Northern Ireland enters a new phase and younger talents such as Peter McDonald, Martin Mooney, and Sinéad Morrissey come to maturity in post-ceasefire, post-Belfast Agreement Ireland, Carson's work remains exemplary; in Auden's words for Yeats, "A way of happening, a mouth." [42]

"'That Blank Mouth'; Secrecy, Shibboleths, and Silence in Northern Irish Poetry," was first published in *Journal of Modern Literature* XXV, 1 (Fall 2001), pp. 1-16. © Indiana University Press, 2002.

NOTES

1   Dillon Johnston, *The Poetic Economies of England and Ireland, 1912-2000* (Basingstoke: Palgrave, 2001), p. xiv.

2   Johnston, p. 180.

3   Seamus Heaney, *The Haw Lantern* (London: Faber and Faber, 1987), p. 17.

4   Flann O'Brien, *The Best of Myles* (London: Grafton Books, 1987), p. 262. Hereafter referred to parenthetically in the text as Best of Myles. It is unclear whether "Shean O Duibhir" and "Sheán O Duíbhir" are intended to be the same person.

5   *The Critical Writings of James Joyce,* ed. Ellsworth Mason and Richard Ellmann (London:

Faber and Faber, 1959), p. 198. Hereafter referred to parenthetically in the text as *Critical Writings*.

6   Craig Raine, "Babylonish Dialects," in *Haydn and the Valve Trumpet* (London: Picador, 2000 [1st ed., 1990]), p. 89.

7   James Joyce, *Finnegans Wake* (Harmondsworth: Penguin, 1992), p. 175.

8   Christopher Ricks, "Andrew Marvell: 'Its Own Resemblance,'" in *The Force of Poetry* (Oxford: Clarendon Press, 1984), pp, 34-35.

9   Samuel Beckett, *The Beckett Trilogy: Molloy, Malone Dies, The Unnamable* (London: Pan, 1979), p. 181.

10 Cf J,H Andrews, "Notes for a Future Edition of Brian Friel's *Translations*", *Irish Review*, XIII, (1992/93), pp. 93-106.

11 Brian Friel, *Translations* (Faber and Faber, 1983), p. 15. Hereafter referred to parenthetically in the text as *Translations*.

12 Seamus Heaney, *Wintering Out* (Faber and Faber, 1972), pp. 16, 26. Hereafter referred to parenthetically in the text as *Wintering Out*.

13 W.J. McCormack, "Seamus Heaney's Preoccupations," in *The Battle of the Books* (Gigginstown: The Lilliput Press, 1984), p. 37.

14 Among the many critics to have written about Heaney's place-name poems are Tom Paulin and Graham Martin, "Seamus Heaney's 'Broagh,'" *The English Review*, II (1992), pp. 28-9; Clair Wills, *Improprieties: Politics and Sexuality in Northern Irish Poetry* (Oxford University Press, 1993), pp. 98-101; David Lloyd, *Anomalous States: Irish Writing and the Post-Colonial Moment* (Dublin: The Lilliput Press, 1993), pp. 24-26; Neil Corcoran, *The Poetry of Seamus Heaney: A Critical Study* (Faber and Faber, 1998 [2nd edition]), pp. 43-49; and John Goodby, *Irish Poetry since 1950* (Manchester University Press, 2000), pp. 154-58.

15 Corcoran, p. 46 (hereafter referred to parenthetically in the text as *The Poetry of Seamus Heaney*). C.I. Macafee's ground-breaking *Concise Ulster Dictionary* (Oxford University Press, 1996) gives "brough" or "broo" as an English naturalization of *bruach*, although among the other meanings listed for "broo" are "a witch who can turn into a hare," "the edge of a potato ridge," and "unemployment benefit," suggesting that madcap polysemousness, too, is shared by Gaelic and Ulster-Scots traditions (see the discussion of Carson's prose poem "Farset" for more on Gaelic polysemousness).

16 Philip Larkin, *Collected Poems,* ed. Anthony Thwaite (Faber and Faber, 1988), p. 104. For a comparison of Heaney and Larkin that touches on "Broagh" see James Booth, "Larkin, Heaney and the Poetry of Place." in James Booth, ed., *New Larkins for Old: Critical Essays* (Basingstoke: Macmillan, 2000), pp. 190-212.

17 Seamus Heaney, *Opened Ground: Poems 1966-1996* (Faber and Faber, 1998), p. 85. The pamphlet of prose poems from which "England's Difficulty" is taken, *Stations* (Belfast: Ulsterman Publications, 1975), has never been reprinted.

18 Neil Corcoran, "A Languorous Cutting Edge: Muldoon versus Heaney?" in *Poets of Modern Ireland* (Cardiff: University of Wales Press, 1999), pp. 121-36 (136). 19 Paul Muldoon, *Quoof* (Faber and Faber, 1983), p. 17. Hereafter referred to parenthetically in the text as Quoof.

20 The Special Air Service (SAS) and Royal Ulster Constabulary (RUC) are, respectively, a British special forces unit and a traditionally Protestant-dominated police force; the presence of both in South Armagh has long been a source of Republican grievance.

21 Tom Herron, "Contemporary Irish Poetry and the Dispersed Body," in Colin Graham and Richard Kirkland, ed. *Ireland and Cultural Theory: The Mechanics of Authenticity* (Macmillan, 1999), p. 204.

22 *Cf.* Toby Harnden, *'Bandit Country': The IRA and South Armagh* (London: Hodder & Stoughton, 1999), pp. 211-24.

23 "Talking to People in South Armagh, by Captain Robert Nairac," appendix to Toby Harnden, pp. 370-71.

24 "Third Epistle to Timothy," *Hay* (Faber and Faber, 1998), p. 99. Hereafter referred to parenthetically in the text as *Hay*. For more on *Hay*, see my "An Irish Poet in America," *Raritan*, XVIII (1999), pp. 145-57, and for an account of Gaelic motifs in Muldoon, see my "The Aistriúchán Cloak: Paul Muldoon and the Irish Language," *New Hibernia Review*, V (2001), pp. 123-34.

25 For more on Anketell Moutray, see Ruth Dudley Edwards, *The Faithful Tribe* (London: Harper Collins, 2000 [2nd ed.]), p. 37. Edward's (highly partisan) study notes the political use of the Irish language in the Gaelicization of Republican spokesmen's names (for instance, Brendan McKenna/ Breandán MacCionniath), "so as to irritate unionists," although in the case of disgraced Republican Seán MacStiofáin, Edwards observes the tendency by Republicans to "downgrade ... him back to his original name," John Stephenson (n., p. 364).

26 Muldoon's line may also echo Austin Clarke's resolution to remove "the clapper from the bell of rhyme," a line singled out for mockery by Samuel Beckett in his "Recent Irish Poetry" (in *Disjecta: Miscellaneous Writings and a Dramatic Fragment*, London: John Calder, 1983, p. 72).

27 *The Irish for No*, Gallery Press, 1987, p. 49. Hereafter referred to parenthetically in the text as *Irish for No*.

28 Neil Corcoran, "One Step Forward, Two Steps Back: Ciaran Carson's *The Irish for No*," in Corcoran, ed., *The Chosen Ground: Essays on the Contemporary Poetry of Northern Ireland* (Bridgend: Seren, 1992), p. 231.

29 Edward Thomas, *Collected Poems* (Faber and Faber, 1988), p. 104.

30 *Belfast Confetti* (Dublin: Gallery Press, 1989), p. 11. Hereafter referred to parenthetically in the text as *Belfast Confetti*.

31 Lewis Carroll, *Alice's Adventures in Wonderland/ Through the Looking Glass* (Oxford University Press, 1998), p.218.

32 Carson had previously used this phrase in his first collection, *The New Estate and Other Poems* (Gallery, 1988 [1st ed., 19761), p. 32.

33 *Cf.* the mirror imagery in "Loaf," also from *Belfast Confetti*.

34 *Cf.* "Campaign" for a similar treatment of identity as something determined externally and through violence: the question "Who exactly was he?" is answered after torture by the interrogated man being "told ... [w]hat he was" and "shot ... nine times" *(Irish for No*, p. 36).

35 Ian Duhig's poem "From the Irish" from *The Bradford Count* offers a further example of the same joke (Newcastle upon Tyne: Bloodaxe Books, 1991, p. 9).

36 Constitutionally Irish remains the first language of the Irish Republic.

37 Goodby, p. 295.

38 *First Language* (Gallery Press, 1993), pp. 12, 13, 16.

39 *Opera et Cetera* (Gallery Press, 1996), p. 11. Hereafter referred to parenthetically in the text as *Opera et Cetera.*

40 Compare "Opus 14": "Spokesman for censored political party spoke in someone else's lip-synch / So perfectly, you'd think it was the man himself, though much of this is double-think" *(First Language, p. 31).*

41 Carson had glanced at the same theme in "Opus Operandi" ("the shibboleths of *aitch* and *haitch: First Language, p.60).*

42 Auden, "In Memory of W.B. Yeats," in Edward Mendelson, ed., The English Auden: Poems, Essays and Dramatic Writings 1927-1939 (London: Faber and Faber, 1977), p. 242.

Nine-and-Fifty Swans: Glimpses of Nature in Recent Irish Poetry

Pat Boran

As a 'townie', born and bred, in my late teens I moved directly to the city, without any extended intervening period in what in Ireland is often called "the country". Without real first-hand experience of "the country", of wild or liminal landscapes and habitats, I suppose I have always fed my appetite for a working knowledge of the natural world, not just with occasional meandering walks, in the style of the lazier of the Romantic poets (sandwich, newspaper, and maybe an iPod tucked discreetly into a bag), but by turning to poems. Poems, more than any other kind of writing, seemed to be able to describe the natural world, and I read them for the information they often managed to convey almost as much as I read them for their insight.

Some of the first poems I ever felt drawn to, then drawn back to, were, not unnaturally, about our creaturely co-habitants: the monk's cat, Pangur Bán; the blackbird singing beyond the monastery window; An Bunnán Buí / The Yellow Bittern, dead of thirst on the road. And, of course, Yeats's many swans. In poetry as in life, birds and animals are often our first encounter with the notion of soul in the natural world, the suggestion that the world is, as posited by James Lovelock among others, a living organism. Were it not for such poetry, in fact, many of us townies who grew up with our backs to the country might never have stopped to glance over our shoulders at what we were missing. Poetry is one of the few places where we are invited to commune with and closely observe the natural world.

YEATS'S SWANS

In the famous *The Wild Swans at Coole,* W.B. Yeats apparently takes great pains to count the nine-and-fifty swans he came upon one day on Coole waters, yet the number troubles me more each time I read the poem. Are we to believe the many critics who interpret the number (59) as signifying 29 pairs (58) and one solitary swan on its own—a reference to the poet in his own solitude? Dedicated birdwatchers will argue that the Whooper swans Yeats would have seen at Coole are in fact "non-breeders", and that swans do not in fact form lasting pairs, despite the many suggestions to the contrary throughout literature. Of course, Yeats could have been consciously referring to the popular image of the faithful, mating-for-life swan, but if so surely nature poem and veiled self-portrait are two different things, two mutually exclusive categories? I'm happy to report now that I'm not so sure. Indeed it might be said that what separates a poem from any other form of writing on the same subject is that the poem *must* proceed in at least two directions at once; and from such tensions do the finest derive their power.

CARRIGSKEEWAUN

I have never been to Carrigskeewaun, Co. Mayo, but I have been to the Carrigskeewaun described in Michael Longley's poetry and know it is more than a linguistic construction. In contemporary Irish poetry Longley is probably the poet most celebrated for his meticulous attention to flora and fauna, in particular the flora and fauna of Co. Mayo where he spends a good deal of his time. Even a cursory glance over his beautifully delicate work will yield riches for the armchair naturalist such as myself. But Longley's work is complex, allusive, cross-referencing: "the nature poetry fertilising the war poetry" as he has put it (in conversation with the American critic Jody Allen Randolph).

> "My nature writing is my most political. In my Mayo poems I am not trying to escape from political violence. I want the light from Carrigskeewaun to irradiate the northern darkness. Describing the world in a meticulous way is a consecration and a stay against damaging dogmatism."

On the subject of Irish nature poetry, in the same interview Longley points out: "Irish nature poetry has only recently got under way—compared with the English tradition. What we have mostly had here is more the poetry of rural community."

This distinction between a poetry of rural community and one of the natural world can certainly be applied to a figure like Patrick Kavanagh, the 'farmer poet' of Monaghan whose relationship to the land was expressed through his inherited or given role, subsequently rejected, as son and servant of that land. Kavanagh is a rural poet but few would describe him as a nature poet; Longley's is an urban, even urbane, voice, yet he is nature poet to the core, to the fingertips. It is not just subject matter, it would seem, but the adopted viewpoint or imposed distance which distinguishes nature poetry from the poetry of rural community.

THE HILLS OF DONEGAL

Rural community certainly features in the work of Francis Harvey, a poet born in Enniskillen, Co. Fermanagh who has made a life's work out of his response to his adopted Donegal, its stony shorelines and stark mountains in particular. Harvey is an attentive but far from passive watcher of natural miracles and wonders. As Moya Cannon puts it in her Introduction to his 2007 *Collected Poems*:

"The rendered beauty of the landscapes which he sees
with a painter's eye is all the more convincing because he
does not flinch from the harshness of the granite
landscapes or from the material poverty of the lives lived
by the sheep farmers who cling to them."

What Cannon admires, along with Harvey's hallmark "vividness
and lucidity" (born of early morning hill-walking "when every
detail of a mountainside is cast into relief"), is the same kind of
very literal focus that distinguishes Longley's finest work. "One
would be tempted to say that Francis Harvey's work combines the
passion for precision of a naturalist and the yearning for grace of a
poet, except for the fact that a passion for precision, for naming, is
also part of the bedrock of poetry."

This idea that precision itself might be the link between the
work of the naturalist and that of the poet is one that can be found
centuries ago in the wonderful marginalia of the illuminated
manuscript tradition (the monks placing birdsong and the word of
the Lord on the same sheet and therefore, implicitly, on the same
level of importance). One might be surprised to meet any Irish
poet who has not been moved and inspired at some point in his or
her development by these same small nature/spiritual moments in
the sometimes far louder and more clamorous cannon of Irish
verse.

Which brings me to the perhaps inevitable point that good
nature poetry will have about it, for want of a better description, a
spiritual dimension, in the sense perhaps that even the smallest
encounters or perceptions it describes may be seen to hold huge
implications for the poet.

BIRDS

Birds, in particular, seem called to this role as messengers between
the immediate known and the greater even mysterious dimensions
of our existence. Mirrors perhaps of some aspect of the troubled or

hidden self, they are in no shortage in poetry anywhere, and certainly not in Irish poetry. One thinks of Mad Sweeney, of the Buile Shuibhne myth, who has attracted a great many poets, standing as he seems to do between the world of human order and that thing we call the 'wild', at once outside of us and, as he forces us to acknowledge, within ourselves.

The donning of masks is again part of it, as it was for Yeats. Seamus Heaney has made the point in relation to his own *Sweeney Astray*, perhaps the definitive modern version of the myth. "I think a myth has to come up in you unconsciously and be discovered in you," he says. "And I've discovered something of Sweeney in me." This kind of discovery is of course part of the process of poetic seeing, by which I mean something more than just imaginative seeing, or a kind of projection of self; something far subtler and more complex.

THE NATURE POET AS WITNESS

Where Longley's nature writing somehow provides a balance for his historically-informed poems, and Heaney and others turn by times to myth as a kind of looking glass, neither features prominently in the work of Mark Roper, an English-born poet longtime resident in Co Kilkenny (half his life now) whose witness is almost exclusively of the spiritual kind, a link perhaps between the Irish monastic tradition and the poet-naturalists of his home country, exemplified by Erasmus Darwin, grandfather of the better known Charles. Indeed, Roper's poems sometimes appear to blur the distinction Longley refers to between English and Irish 'traditions' or angles of approach. His eye is keenly concerned with the natural world, though much of his poetry has an almost domestic (though far from drawing room) feel to it. If the Romantic poets fled from what might be termed "civilized nature", scaling mountains for their inspiration, Roper's is more likely to be found in the unkempt grass at the bottom of the garden, or, indeed, in the garden shed itself, as in the poem 'Angel' in which the apparition of a heavenly creature reads as pure nature poem by any other name.

> An angel showed me its wing
> in a field at the back of the house.
> It was leathery inside, vein-knotted,
> welted with stitchmarks and scars.
> There were fleas in the feathers
> which it made me catch and crush.
> You could feel the shafts buried
> deep in the skin, like great nails.

If Roper's nature poems may be said to have a distinctly spiritual quality to them, here is a poem that is spiritual in subject matter but to which he brings the kind of precise attention one might expect, and wish for, in nature poetry.

In one of his finest short poems (and there are many to choose from in *Even So,* his 2008 New and Selected Poems), a dead swallow is seen as "A spent firework / on the lawn", a first impression that suggests some kind of human interference in the bird's death, a subtle invitation to look and think again of our role as custodians of the planet.

Retreating ever more each day—as most of us appear to be—from the domain of nature, visits by birds and other creatures often provide our only access to the uncivilized world. The visitation of birds, or birdsong, has the power to charm and centre us, like almost no other sound, and our fascination with it goes back to, and no doubt much further than, those fleeting references in the margins and "The little bird / that whistled shrill / from the nib of / its yellow bill" as Ciaran Carson's version of the famous poem has it. What we hear in such song and perceive in such visits is in part the message of the bird, in part a message we are sending to ourselves.

A good nature poet is, we might say, like a guide who gently taps the glass screens we are busy erecting between the world and ourselves, and beckons us to follow. The "careful excitement" or "sense of privilege" which Carol Rumens remarks upon in Mark

Roper's work, or the painstaking precision with which Michael Longley seems to weave his poems, results in lyrics that might be said to sing their little hearts out on the margins of considerably darker material.

In Ciaran Berry's remarkable debut, *Sphere of Birds* (Gallery Press, 2008), the poem 'For the Birds' includes encounters with petrels, kittiwakes and black-headed gulls that feed on the remains of a hare and which, among other things, help the poet

> to understand a little more what the dead mean
> to the living, why every St. Stephen's Day
> of that decade we lived on the outskirts of town
>
> the same three freckled cousins, wearing straw hats
> and masks, would bring to our front door
> a single wren.

Later in the same poem he considers

> those blue tits Keats shot
> to clear the air a few days after his brother
>
> coughed up phlegm flecked with blood for the last time.

In a poem which includes meditations on topics as diverse as surgery, community, religion and death, Berry glimpses the almost invisible links between all of them, and in doing so implicitly defends a kind of connected dreaming which is all too often dismissed as "for the birds".

These days, Irish poets might be said to be "for the birds" in the other common meaning of that phrase, *for* them as one might be for a football team, the underdog or victim. If the blackbirds of medieval manuscripts seemed once to sing for Irish poets, one might argue that Irish poets have now been drafted to sing for the blackbird and its endangered kind.

DISTRACTION, NOISE AND NATURE

Seán Lysaght, in a recent posting on his internet blog (http://stonechat.blogspot.com/) finds himself wondering about Edmund Spenser, provoked by Spenser's use (in *The Faerie Queene)* of the word 'mizzle' to mean a light rain, a variant of which he has also noticed in Seamus Heaney's 'Bog Oak' (*Wintering Out, 1972*). "Moving to Ireland did not," Lysaght says, "make Spenser a more rural poet: if anything, his isolation from the natives detracted from his earlier affinity with nature and the land." *The Faerie Queene* turned out to be "more abstract and ideological" than Spenser's earlier poetry which is actually "very close to the countryside". Maybe absence, or distance, does indeed make the heart grow fonder; Wordsworth's definition of poetry is, after all, emotion "recollected in tranquility", that is after the fact. And if not physical distance, for others some distraction or routine duty seems often to be necessary before the muse or singing bird of poetry might find access and make itself heard.

Many years ago, the poet John F. Deane spoke to a writing workshop about his method of getting a poem clear of the internal distractions and barriers and onto the page. Did he need absolute silence, or music, when he was writing, one of my fellow students wanted to know. "I turn the television all the way up," he gleefully responded, enjoying the shock on our faces. Deane's questioning, indeed questing Catholic vision is intensely interested in the natural world; where Longley's nature poetry might engage with politics as its human-weighted counterbalance, for Deane nature and religious faith are inextricable. But what is clear and available to the conscious self is often out of reach to poetry, and vice versa, and for a subject to manifest itself in a poem it is often necessary for the poet to be looking the other way.

NATURAL SOLITUDE

Another west of Ireland poet, Patrick Deeley is a poet for whom, in the words of Fred Johnston *(Books Ireland)* "the raw immensity of the rural will, one suspects, always hold the ultimate imaginative fascination". Deeley's poems show what Brendan Kennelly has called "an almost atavistic identification with the lives of untamed creatures" *(Sunday Independent)*, a muscularity, earthedness and earthiness which Deeley's poetry has lost little of, despite his living in Dublin where he's worked as a school principal for many years.

The poem 'Dandelions' from his recent collection *The Bones of Creation* (Dedalus Press, 2008) concludes:

> There seemed
> to be room then, abundance of
> wildflower places, but these were weeds
> still, they brought me to my knees,
> I cursed tillage, the big darkness
> fell, the first stars twinkled,
> the world wheeled by, suiting itself
> until I forgot and was forgotten, and grew
> alone, and knew this was natural.

If one senses by times the anger of Patrick Kavanagh, and something of the spiritual reaching of Deane, the closing note here is very much Deeley's own: not resigned, or bitter, or especially suffering any longer, but abandoned, cut loose, set free, in exile, as so many of us find ourselves to be, close to home.

'INTEMPERATE LOOKING'

The challenge of truly seeing, and representing, is an almost insurmountable one, but a determined outward gaze might be said to be part of the technique of another Fermanagh-born poet, Mary Montague, whose second much-admired collection of poems,

Tribe, was published last year. Having studied Genetics and Botany at Queen's University, Montague has "the trained eye of the natural scientist and the impassioned soul of the poet", as Eva Bourke puts it, working together to produce what Ted Deppe calls "accomplished acts of 'intemperate looking'".

Blake's little lamb and Tiger are close by, but so too is Rilke's Panther pacing back and forth in his cage, and all the creatures we have caged, physically, or mentally, by reducing or withdrawing from them into a world of our own making. Despite their determined precision and focus, like the equestrian artist George Stubbs, subject of some of the finest of them, the poems even so recognize their inadequacy: "How beauty blinds," Montague writes, "disguises its distress" ('Anatomy of the Horse').

YEATS AND SWANS, AGAIN—A SHORT DETOUR

Is it in fact possible to write nature poetry, poetry that is faithful to the natural world? And aren't poets really the last people we should count on for objective fact? Was Yeats, for that matter, ever really out counting swans, or was he just away somewhere inside of himself, counting the symbols of swans, the reflections of swans on the troubled waters of his own thoughts?

A fascinating book, *Yeats at Work,* by Curtis B. Bradford (W.W. Norton, 1978) provides a possible answer. In this truly revealing volume, Bradford traces the development of a small number of Yeats's poems, recording their first tentative appearances in journals together with the subsequent revisions the poet was to make to them before, and sometimes after, their first appearances in print.

Happily for this undisciplined but sometimes lucky reader, the three main drafts, and further sub-drafts, which Yeats made of *The Wild Swans at Coole* are included, complete with the poet's markings, second thoughts, deletions and replacements. One notices, of course, the subtle ways in which Yeats achieves what Bradford calls "the management of his persona", determinedly keeping himself out of the opening of the poem, instead first setting the scene into which he was about to make his entrance: "The trees are in their autumn beauty, / The woodland paths are dry …"). One notices too the way Yeats is constantly revising earlier versions of a line such as "I have trod with a lighter tread", first by redirecting the reader's attention to some parallel movement ("I did not turn with *this* slow tread"— my italics) and, in the final version, separating the poet and his effect on the scene entirely, moving the words "I" and "trod" (subject and verb) three full lines apart, so as to draw our attention away from the poet and instead to precisely where he wanted it at this point, that is to the swans themselves:

> All's changed since I, *hearing at twilight,*
> *The first time on this shore,*
> *The bell-beat of their wings above my head,*
> Trod with a lighter tread."
> (again, my italics)

If anything, the laying out like this, side by side as it were, of the various versions of the poem only seems to amplify the strange dedication to counting, even to *accounting* in all of its many meanings, which features so prominently, and the powerful significance for Yeats of numbers themselves. (There are, for instance, no les than seven version of the lines which will eventually become "The nineteenth autumn has come upon me / Since I first made my count", only the number itself remaining unchanged throughout, as if it were haunting the poet so much that the syntax around it had become disturbed, unsettled by its persistence.)

The fascination of a close-up reading of a poet as dexterous as Yeats can itself bring considerable pleasure, but should not detain us too long here. What is perhaps more important is that, out of the corner of our eyes, we notice in the almost parallel, almost mirror worlds of these rewrites, a slight flicker of doubt with regard to the swans, the entrance of the insubstantial, the impossible to substantiate, that is often the real lure for the poet's imagination and the inquisitive reader's attention. For there, between the first and third revisions, during which "the bell-beat of their wings" morphs into "the slow clamor (sic) of their wings" and finally "their clamorous wings", some shadow, one might say, seems to pass over the creatures themselves.

"I have Coole's fifty nine / Mysterious, beautiful," Yeats sets out his stall in what Bradford designates as draft A2, later adding a drop of magic to the number by rephrasing it as "nine-and-fifty swans" with its echo of biblical language. But then, without warning, the number of swans seems to fluctuate, becoming "five and forty dream creatures" in draft C1, the ranks swelling marginally further in draft C3 with "I have numbered all the brilliant creatures / And I am but heart sore / I have counted five and forty two" before ending up back with the original number, 59, or nine-and-fifty, in the version which has since become fact:

> The trees are in their autumn beauty,
> The woodland paths are dry,
> Under the October twilight the water
> Mirrors a still sky;
> Upon the brimming water among the stones
> Are nine-and-fifty Swans.

Was Yeats just distracted for a moment, or for two or three moments, his mind on something else temporarily more pressing, like spelling, for instance, which he had terrible trouble with? Did he write five and forty, and five and forty two (ie 47), because the swans were constantly moving about, one masking the other in bright plumage just as an actor will sometimes inadvertently plunge another into shade? Whatever the answer, the questions has implications beyond the reach of this particular mystery. Did Yeats make it all up, the nine-and-fifty swans, the clamorous wings of that particular moment of impression, insight and flight? In *The Lake Isle of Inisfree*, for that matter, did he really yearn for bean-rows, did he give a whit for bean-rows or rows of anything else, or was it the number nine, for whatever occult reason, he was really, secretly, interested in? Were those famous opening lines any more faithful to his vision than the parody an elderly friend of mine made some ten years ago when, using his new Senior Citizen travel pass for the first time (to take a bus to the Willie Clancy Summer School in Co. Clare) he stood up in the pub to announce, in stentorian tones: "I will arise and go now, and go to Ennis—free!" In short, was Yeats counting swans, or just pretending to count them, as perhaps a way to keep his undeniably flighty imagination busy for a while on solid ground?

If so, it's no bad way for a poet to work, if the evidence be Yeats achievement. For the true poet is always looking for what the great 1st century Chinese poet Lu Chi called "the cage of form" in which to catch and scrutinize reality, subjective and objective. The nine-and-fifty swans are Yeats's assistants, his fellows and companions in the quest; they still his tread, and his mind, long enough for him to see the brimming water, to hear the clamorous wings, to sense the proximity of the day on which he will awake "to find they have flown away".

PRECISION AND ACCURACY

In truth, Yeats himself has given us fair warning of what the presence of swans might signify in his work, through 'Nineteen Hundren and Nineteen', 'Leda and the Swan', and numerous other works, but directly in 'Coole Park and Ballylee' (1931) where he writes of yet another swan seen taking to the sky above a lake:

> Another emblem there! That stormy white
> But seems a concentration of the sky.

Perhaps Yeats's reference to nine-and-fifty swans should, if anything, more fairly be called an illusion, an invention, a vision (to use his own favoured word) rather than an inaccuracy. Perhaps precision and accuracy may not after all be the same thing—the precision of the hunter's aim, for instance, does not guarantee the accuracy of the shot when it reaches its target. Yeats stacks up so much precision on this occasion (count them, nine-and-fifty, he seems to say) that we almost dare not doubt his vision.

For a depiction of a swan that truly has no comparison in recent Irish nature poetry, one need look no further than the poem 'Swan in Winter' by Eamon Grennan, (*So It Goes,* Gallery Press, 1995), a wonderfully precise and hugely affecting poem which moves from the death of a swan to deaths closer to home:

> There is this enormous white sleep.
> No marks visible on the soft body
> sprawled on saltgrass in a few inches
> of rocking water, the neck
> limp as water and flopping back
> when you lift and let go, hauling it
> out to the solid ground of shells
> and seawrack, twilight lights winking
> at the wide mouth of the Sound.

No idealized depiction of a swan here, but:

> Orange beak, black legs and feet
> blatant in that mass of white:

and later

> There is this solid feel of bone
> inside the wing you've opened,
> a hinged brightness wide as
> a whitewashed wall, the life
> seeped out of it, your own hinge-
> winged hand the stronger, this huge case
> hollow and heavy, immense, bereft,
> but ruling in its white absence
> the whole foreshore:

And Grennan finds, in this happened-upon corpse, images of the
death of a mother and father, and bridging between the two the
image of his own hand, hinge-winged, as he puts it, like a hand
held up to the light of inspection which will reveal the same
creaturely structures as are all too evident in the dead bird.

Many readers, like myself, sense deep links between poetry and the
natural world, as if the former were a kind of song of the latter. The
subject of poetry can move far indoors, far inside the constant low
drone of the self, but its energy derives from its links to what is
beyond it. The very language of our interior conversations formed
itself in the living world. The nature poet may take to the hills of
Donegal, the rivers and boglands of Mayo, the shoreline of the
Howth estuary—or simply stand and gaze into the field beyond
the fence, the grass before the fence, the bulbs and weeds already
firing themselves into action underfoot: the term 'nature poetry',
like 'life experience', is perhaps just another oxymoron.

The Irish word *dinnseanchas* reminds us that every place has a
story, and that every story has its origin in a place. From the
sadness-steeped Zen blues of Dermot Healy—

> Oh the road to Belmullet—
> you'll not be on it,
> My love and my darling.
>
> Oh the road to Clonmany—
> The green finch
> Is all that there is.
> ('The Road')

—to the bilingual haiku of Gabriel Rosenstock

> i bhfolach sa dorchadas
> na crainn a dhúisíonn
> dár maidin

> hidden in the dark
> the trees that awaken
> to our morning

that sense of place singing is everywhere. Tom MacIntyre's short poem, 'Sun-Bathing' (*A Glance Will Tell You and A Dream Confirm*, Dedalus Press, 1994), in which a bird alights on the reclining poet's big toe, reminds us of how trapped we are in our own world-view: "A first / for me," he says, "can't speak for the bird".

The links between bird and poet, flight and poem, can be found in poetry of all times and places, from the muse-like function of the nightingale in Aristophanes' 'The Birds' ("Come, you, who play spring melodies upon the harmonious flute, lead off our anapests") to "the calligraphy of swallows / on a page of cloud" in the title poem of Vona Groarke's *Flight* (Gallery Press, 2002). The task is an apparently impossible one—how to record the interplay of external and internal natures—but all the more commanding for that.

The recognition that the natural world—dwarfing of us in so many of our activities—is also finite, fragile and endangered by these same activities is part of any good nature poetry. A good poet is always a kind of gardener or curator, on his knees in the garden of language, tending the orchard of images, filling the basket of form. Perhaps it is for this reason that in Ireland we may call someone a poet who has never have tried, or even thought, to write a line—as if 'poet' and 'maker of poems' were related but distinct identities. Either way there are no shortage of poets who commit to language their interaction with the natural world in all its manifestations, the many figures I have already mentioned, the many others I might have named had the nine-and-fifty swans on this occasion rearranged themselves differently before me, on the brimming water or the flickering cloudscape of the page.

This essay is a shortened version of a lecture given at the Yeats Winter School in Sligo, 24 January, 2009.

The Future of Irish Poetry?

RICHARD TILLINGHAST

F ew readers would question Seamus Heaney's position as the
preeminent Irish poet of the second half of the 20th century.
But few of us have a good grasp of who his successors may
be, which poets those with an interest in Irish writing might want
to read next, which poets readers in future years are likely to see as
filling the shoes of Heaney and his peers. Because he does have
peers—poets just as rewarding as Heaney for those who love poetry
but equally below the radar for readers who have room on their
reading lists for only one poet at a time of literature from a country
other than their own. Heaney is, and has been, but one of a group
of talented poets to emerge from Northern Ireland in the sixties.
He tends to be grouped with Michael Longley, Derek Mahon and
James Simmons, with younger Northern poets such as Mebdh
McGuckian, Paul Muldoon and Ciaran Carson following in their
footsteps. And beyond these names, Ireland both north and south
continues to distinguish itself in the field of poetry.

In 2005 Wake Forest University Press published the first
volume in a projected series of anthologies of Irish poetry. The
poets chosen by Jefferson Holdridge for this anthology are Harry
Clifton, born in 1952; Dennis O'Driscoll, born in 1954; David
Wheatley, born in 1970; Sinéad Morrissey, born in 1972; and
Caitríona O'Reilly, born in 1973. Perhaps this book provides as
good a platform as any to talk about what has been happening

recently on the poetry scene in Ireland.

It is illuminating to read these poets against a background of those who preceded them. One thing W.B. Yeats, Louis MacNeice, Patrick Kavanagh and Seamus Heaney, four major poets in the generations preceding the current one, had in common was their preoccupation with their native country both as a nation and as a place. This is not surprising, but when asked to define Ireland, each would have given a different answer.

Yeats as a young man delved into Irish mythology and folklore as a member of the Celtic Revival movement, dreamed of an independent Ireland, and was a major participant in the effort to define the young nation once it came into existence, as a Senator in the Free State and spokesman for broad and tolerant national self-definition which took into account the diversity of religions and ethnic strains that had gone into creating modern Ireland. Yeats's definition of Ireland ultimately lost out to the nationalist fervour that ushered in the repressive climate of de Valera's Ireland, an insular society which managed to outlaw divorce and contraception and ban almost every major work of modern Irish literature.

Though most of his career was spent in London, where we worked for the BBC, Louis MacNeice experienced the excesses of religious intolerance first-hand as the son of an Anglican clergyman growing up in an Ulster characterized by bigotry and ignorance on both sides of the cultural divide. Commenting on the old cliché about Ireland as a "land of saints and scholars", he wrote in 'Autumn Journal':

> The land of scholars and saints:
>   Scholars and saints my eye, the land of ambush,
> Purblind manifestoes, never-ending complaints,
>   The born martyr and the gallant ninny;
> The grocer drunk with the drum,

> The land-owner shot in his bed, the angry voices
> Piercing the broken fanlight in the slum,
> The shawled woman weeping at the garish altar.

Kavanagh's focus on the local can be seen as a reaction against Yeats's lofty rhetoric and grand ideas about the emerging Irish nation. Unlike Yeats, Kavanagh just went about his business as a writer and did not engage in polemics. Historians tell us that the idea of Ireland as an entity, a focus of individual identity, began to jell only with the drive toward Home Rule and independence in the 19th century. Most Irish people would have been more likely to identify themselves, except when travelling abroad, in terms of locality within Ireland rather than as broadly Irish—as a Kerryman, or a Sligo woman or Connemara woman, or a Dub; each of these identifications has a particularly flavour to it, just as in the United States you would never confuse a Mississippian with a downeasterner from Maine or a New Yorker. Kavanagh, a farmer in County Monaghan before he migrated down to Dublin, was a firm believer in the value of the local. There is a Zen-like simplicity in his assertion that "To know fully even one field or one lane is a lifetime's experience ... A gap in a hedge, a smooth rock surfacing a narrow lane, a view of a woody meadow, the stream at the junction of four small fields—these are as much as a man can fully experience". His sonnet 'Epic' is worth quoting in full for the confident and sly way it comments on the centrality of the local:

> I have lived in important places, times
> When great events were decided, who owned
> That half a rood of rock, a no-man's land
> Surrounded by our pitchfork-armed claims.
> I heard the Duffys shouting 'Damn your soul'
> And old McCabe stripped to the waist, seen
> Step the plot defying blue cast-steel—
> 'Here is the march along these iron stones'.
> That was the year of the Munich bother. Which
> Was more important? I inclined
> To lose my faith in Ballyrush and Gortin
> Till Homer's ghost came whispering to my mind.

> He said: I made the Iliad from such
> A local row. Gods make their own importance.

Louis MacNeice in *The Closing Album* wrote a poem with some interesting parallels to 'Epic'. In 'Cushenden', as in Kavanagh's 'Epic' with its tongue-in-cheek mention of "the Munich bother", the war is referred to slyly and ironically, but more ambiguously than in the Monaghan man's poem. 'Cushenden' (a town in County Antrim) introduces us to "Limestone and basalt and a whitewashed house / With passages of great stone flags" where everything is cosy and serene. It could be nothing more than an evocation of a house in a seaside village in Northern Ireland until the last two lines of the poem, which bring the BBC into the room. Here are the last two stanzas of the poem:

> Forgetfulness: brass lamps and copper jugs
> And home-made bread and the smell of turf or flax
> And the air a glove and the water lathering easy
> And convolvulus in the hedge.

> Only in the dark green room beside the fire
> With the curtains drawn against the winds and waves
> There is a little box with a well-bred voice:
> What a place to talk of War.

Heaney may be said to have picked up the reins from Kavanagh and to have kept ploughing the same field, only with greater resources and a wider purview. The bluster of 'Epic' is antithetical to Heaney's caution and sense of tact. He has approached the subject of national self-definition indirectly, famously contrasting the American sense of "manifest destiny" which defined itself by pushing farther and farther into the western frontier, in a horizontal movement, to the vertical, introspective direction of the Irish:

> Our pioneers keep striking
> Inwards and downwards,

> Every layer they strip
> Seems camped on before.
> The bogholes might be Atlantic seepage.
> The wet centre is bottomless.

In 'The Haw Lantern' he turns the homely hawberry into an emblematic lantern for the Irish people:

> The wintry haw is burning out of season,
> crab of the thorn, a small light for small people,
> wanting no more from them but that they keep
> the wick of self-respect from dying out,
> not having to blind them with illumination.

If MacNeice, Kavanagh, Heaney and Yeats each defined Ireland differently, still there is an attitude toward their native country that is typical of all of them. It need hardly be said that the sense of place has traditionally been as strong in Ireland as anywhere in the world. The mystique of landscape spoke powerfully to Yeats; it appears early in the poetry written by the young man living in London, dreaming of Sligo, in almost every poem he wrote—'The Stolen Child', for instance:

> Where the wandering water gushes
> From the hills above Glen-Car,
> In pools among the rushes
> That scarce could bathe a star ...

And one cannot fail to respond to the sense of place in middle and late Yeats; in 'My House' from 'Meditations in Time of Civil War', to give another example:

> An ancient bridge, and a more ancient tower,
> A farmhouse that is sheltered by its wall,
> An acre of stony ground,
> Where the symbolic rose can break in flower,
> Old ragged elms, old thorn innumerable,
> The sound of the rain or sound
> Of every wind that blows ...

One hardly need quote from Heaney and Kavanagh, whose evocations of local landscape are the meat and drink of poetry. Even the work of the acerbic and cosmopolitan MacNeice and Derek Mahon, who was strongly influenced by the older poet, are at times drenched with a love of the landscape, as witness this stanza from MacNeice's 'Train to Dublin':

> I give you the smell of Norman stone, the squelch
> Of bog beneath your boots, the red bog-grass,
> The vivid chequer of the Antrim hills, the trough of dark
> Golden water for the car-horses, the brass
> Belt of serene sun upon the lough.

When we come to the new poets, those included in the Wake Forest anthology, that old sense of Ireland seems to have gone up in smoke. It would seem that now, as a prosperous member of the European Union, host to waves of emigration from Eastern Europe and elsewhere, Ireland is just like everywhere else. Harry Clifton's poetry raises several questions of poetic identity. Is Clifton an Irish poet? Certainly: he was born and educated in Ireland, spent most of his first twenty-five years here. On the other hand, he also lived briefly in South America as a boy, and from the ages of about twenty-five to almost fifty-five he spent more time away from Ireland than in it. He has taught English in Nigeria, England, France and Italy, worked for the Irish Civil Service in refugee aid programs in Thailand, and lived in Paris for many years. In 2004 he returned to this country and now lives again in Dublin. Yet if Beckett was Ireland's first European playwright, Derek Mahon and Harry Clifton may be the country's first European poets.

The sense of rootedness in Ireland as a place is just not present in Clifton's work. That doesn't mean he is lacking in a sense of place—simply that his sense of place attaches more to landscapes like the one evoked in 'The Desert Route', a bizarre, in-between territory near the border between, one supposes, two Saharan countries. The focus on geometry and abstraction in the desert superhighway's "lines of purpose" is characteristic of Clifton's philosophical caste of mind:

> ... the camel trains,
> The slow asphalting gangs
> On the superhighway, laying down
> Lines of purpose, almost merging
> At times, almost parallel,
> Except at the border, where a soldier
> With three stripes, wishing himself elsewhere
> Is waving the landrovers on.

The self in Clifton's poetry is attenuated, impersonal, a kind of philosophical equivalent of the Existentialist figures in Giacometti's sculptures. Clifton's poem 'Reductio' is an homage to the sculptor. But Giacometti's spirit also informs the self presented in 'The Waking Hour':

> ... I float upwards, from my own depths,
> With a woman beside me
> Wondering, wondering am I real
> Or an angel trapped in the glass of a bedside prayer
> And have I come into her life, and will I stay there
>
> With the other objects, nailed to the wall
> Like permanence, or habit,
> Achieving humanity, averaging out
> Between sacred and profane, through the long attritions
> Marriage and work ordain ....

Marriage, too, is one of Clifton's preoccupations. 'The Better Portion' tells of a couple whose harmonious routines are shattered by a sudden eruption from the wife's subconscious, reminiscent of Sylvia Plath's disturbed and disturbing self-discovery when she suddenly found herself able to articulate the depth of her rage toward her dead father. Here are he last two stanzas of the poem:

>   Suddenly
> One evening, she talked a blue streak
> From half-past-eleven
> To four-fifteen, then fell asleep
> Like a stone disappearing into the deep.
> All this comes from nowhere,
>
> He told himself, flabbergasted
> And unmanned, with the working surface
> Of marriage all around him
> To hold on to—heart and head,
> The better portion neither disputed
> In all their years of breaking bread
> Before she emerged, from the underworld.

Intellectuals such as Ignazio Silone, Soren Kierkegaard, Thomas Merton, haunt Clifton's work like familiars; he addresses them, contemplates their lives as object-lessons. Going further back, Saint Augustine ('Reading Saint Augustine') and his world exert a particular fascination:

> As for myself, I was desperate to get back
> Behind Augustine's City of God
> To a time before our time, of plunder and sack,
> Where the word Apocalypse was clearly stated.

The act of reading history, and thinking about history, have seldom been presented so vividly and palpably. He puts this ancient world in the context of his own life:

> Eleven thirty. Carthage and Thagaste
> Long since fallen, knew their gods had failed.
> Alaric and his Huns had stove them in
> Like Rome before them. Adeodatus the bastard
> Of Augustine, and Augustine himself, were dead.
> All that was left, now, was the City of God.
> The orgies, the pomaded boys, the love-ins,
> All were over. Outside, sirens wailed—
> A truck rolled by, the windowglass vibrated.

> Otherwise all was normal. In your room
> Another sentence formed.

The effect of these poems, with their cool surfaces and lack of obvious affect, is a certain disengagement. If we compare Clifton's stance with those of his predecessors, we might wonder why, finally, his poetry feels so different from theirs. Yeats, Kavanagh, MacNeice, Heaney all in their own ways maintain a certain distance and reserve. Perhaps Clifton's work simply shows us how much the world has changed, how glaringly its inequalities, brutality and exploitation impress themselves on someone who has put himself in a position to see first-hand what is happening in other parts of the world—other cultures that MacNeice, Heaney and Kavanagh would seem to have had little interest in, while Yeats mined other cultures such as Byzantium, China and Japan for their mythic value. I have been emphasizing the specifically European identity of these poems. To show how deep and how informed and genuine this identification is, I need to quote one poem in its entirety. To read it in bits and pieces is to miss out on the wealth of connections Clifton is able to make, in bringing to the continent of Europe that bracing and powerful sense of place Kavanagh and Heaney brought to their Irish poems.

TAKING THE WATERS

> There are taps that flow, all day and all night,
> From the depths of Europe,
> Inexhaustible, taken for granted,
>
> Slaking our casual thirsts
> At a railway station
> Heading south, or here in the Abruzzo
>
> Bursting cold from an iron standpipe
> While our blind mouths
> Suck at essentials, straight from the water table.
>
> Our health is too good, we are not pilgrims.
> And the nineteenth century
> Led to disaster. Aix, and Baden Baden—

Where are they now, those ladies with the vapours
Sipping at glasses of hydrogen sulphide
Every morning, while the pump-house piano played

And Russian radicals steamed and stewed
For hours in their sulphur tubs
Plugged in to the cathodes of Revolution?

Real cures, for imaginary ailments—
Diocletian's, or Vespasian's.
History passes, only the waters remain,

Bubbling up, through their carbon sheets,
To the other side of catastrophe
Where we drink, at a forgotten source,

Through the old crust of Europe
Centuries deep, restored by a local merchant
Of poultry and greens, inscribing his name in Latin.

Dennis O'Driscoll brings to his poetry a distinctiveness that could perhaps only be attained by someone who has on the one hand read a tremendous amount of poetry and who on the other is unhampered by an academic study of literature. Commentators on his work tend to stress the latter influence; O'Driscoll studied law and has worked for decades as an Irish civil servant—not stationed abroad like Harry Clifton, but in the heart of Dublin. Part of his distinctiveness is that you will hardly ever encounter in his work the poem-in-a-setting that is a staple of the genre—the kind of writing that begins with the poet positioned in a particular place, where the poem unfolds as a meditation occasioned by that positioning. I open Paul Muldoon's anthology, *Contemporary Irish Poetry*, at random, and the first poem I find is Thomas Kinsella's 'Mirror in February', which begins "The day dawns with scent of must and rain, / Of opened soil, dark trees, dry bedroom air". 'The Other Side' by Seamus Heaney begins, "Thigh-deep in sedge and marigolds / a neighbour laid his shadow / on the stream …"

Many great poems, many good poems have been written, for centuries, in the poem-in-a-setting mode, but perhaps this has become a bit too comfortable a way to proceed. O'Driscoll's poems tend to come at you from out of nowhere, often seemingly prompted by an idea—the idea behind 'Someone', for example, being the unpredictability of death. Here is how it begins:

> someone is dressing up for death today, a change of skirt
>   or tie
> eating a final feast of buttered sliced pan, tea
> scarcely having noticed the erection that was his last
> shaving his face to marble for the icy laying out
> spraying with deodorant her coarse armpit grass
> someone today is leaving home on business
> saluting, terminally, the I who will join in the cortege

Perhaps the first thing one notices about this poem, beyond its boldness of presentation, is its impersonality, its evocation of all these different someones, each saved from abstraction by precise details: "someone's waist will not be marked with elastic in the future / someone is putting out milkbottles for a day that will not come". O'Driscoll's poems are at home with unrealized potentiality—'Spoiled Child', for instance, which begins

> my child recedes inside me
> and need never puzzle where it came from
> or lose a football in the dusty laurel bushes
> or sneak change from my jacket to buy sweets
>
> my child will not engage in active military service
> or make excuses about its school report
> or look up from a picture book, dribbling a pink smile
> or qualify for free glasses or school lunch

Another quality that makes his poetry distinctive is that while many poets project a personality that is strikingly exceptional, O'Driscoll likes to write impersonally about the typical, the ordinary. Perhaps he has absorbed some of the impersonality of his role as a civil servant. 'Misunderstanding and Muzak', presents a typical modern couple who might be residents of any city in the world, no doubt coming from their separate jobs at the end of the working day:

> You are in the Super Valu supermarket
> expecting to meet me at 6:15.
>
> I am in the Extra Valu supermarket
> Expecting to meet you at 6:15.
>
> Danny Boy is calling you down special-offer aisles.
> Johann Strauss is waltzing me down special-offer aisles.

There may be early poems by O'Driscoll that show the influence of Irish exemplars, but I've no evidence of it. The raptures and high rhetoric of Yeats would not suit his temperament, while the rootedness of Kavanagh and Heaney might have seemed a bit too familiar to a young man growing up in the town of Thurles, Co Tipperary. I catch a note of Larkin's hard-bitterness from time to time in O'Driscoll's lines; but on the whole it seems to me that he has gone to school to the Eastern Europeans and the Americans. He would appear to have learned his impersonality and simplicity from translations of poets like Holub, Milosz and Szymborska, and he may have acquired "the common touch" from his reading of American poetry. 'Them and You' deftly summarises the class divide in an Ireland where the beneficiaries of the Celtic Tiger live uneasily side by side with those for whom the new Ireland is no different from the old, only everything is more expensive. Here are the first four couplets:

> They wait for the bus.
> You spray them with puddles.
>
> They queue for curry and chips.
> You phone an order for delivery.

They place themselves under the protection
of the Marian Grotto at the front of their estate.

You put your trust in gilts, managed funds,
income continuation plans.

Through his job with the Customs department of the Irish
government, O'Driscoll has acquired a familiarity with the world
of business, a familiarity he uses to advantage in the long sequence,
The Bottom Line. In the following stanza he constructs a chilling
metaphor for death from that world. You can see here how clearly
he has subverted the familiar emblems of death:

Death, once brushed against,
does not seem in the least
like a stubbly ghost with scythe
reaping dry grass in the graveyard,
but shows up as a brash executive
cutting recklessly across your lane,
lights making eye-contact with yours,
ready to meet head-on as though
by previous appointment; ram home
your car horn like a panic button:
his cellphone's bell will toll for you.

If literature's two great themes are death and love, you won't
find much of the latter here. Love poetry is, in fact, a territory that
Irish writers have approached only with hesitation and reticence. It
is not really surprising that one of Heaney's most forthright
attempts in this genre is called 'The Skunk'! Tenderness enters the
world of O'Driscoll's poetry in a most indirect and qualified way,
in the rather horrifying 'In Memory of Alois Alzheimer', a graphic
description of the gruesome effects of the disease. The last section,
distanced from any personal construance by being printed in
italics, goes as following:

Lie closer to me in the dry sheets
while I can still tell who you are.

Let me declare how much I love you
before our bed is sorely tested.

Love me with drooling toxins, with carbon monoxide,
with rope, with arrows through my heart.

Perhaps I am being presumptuous, but 'Vigil' certainly sounds
like the closest thing to a personal credo we are likely to get from
this quintessentially circumspect poet. Here is part of it, from the
middle of the poem:

> You are alone in the bone-weary tower
> of your bleary-eyed, blinking lighthouse,
> watching the spillage of tide on the shingle inlet.
> You are the single-minded one who hears
> time shaking from the clock's fingertips
> like drops, who watches its hands
> chop years into diced seconds ....

Dennis O'Driscoll has produced an extraordinary body of work
by going to work patiently and quietly on what would appear to be
most ordinary. In the Dublin literary world he is regarded in the
way Samuel Johnson was thought of in eighteenth-century
London. Some of his poems have already achieved the status of
classics.

To include in a single book five poets, two in their fifties, three in
their thirties, does not make for an ideal collection. The reader
implicitly makes comparisons which are not really fair to the
younger poets. Unlike philosophers and mathematicians, few
poets have really found themselves before the age of forty. David
Wheatley had high visibility on the Irish and British literary
scenes as a prolific book reviewer and co-editor of the excellent
magazine *Metre,* which had bases in Dublin, Prague, and the

University of Hull in the UK. The magazine was inclusive and eclectic. Seamus Heaney was listed as a patron. Contributors included poets from three major centres of writing in English: Britain, Ireland and the US.

I have before me an issue from 2004 which I found remaindered in a Dublin bookstore. This issue includes contributions from four of the poets featured in the Wake Forest anthology—Clifton, O'Driscoll, Wheatley and Caitríona O'Reilly—as well as poems by Michael Longley, Robert Pinsky, Anne Stevenson, Ben Sonnenberg, a symposium on Robert Lowell's *Collected Poems,* an essay on Polish poetry by the American poet Charles Altieri, and on and on. What I would have least expected to find is a gathering of essays on the Objectivist poet Carl Rakosi. It would seem that *Metre* ws more informed about American poetry than most readers in America. *Metre's* scope was encyclopaedic.

Poetry has always had its entrepreneurs. Wheatley reminds me of the young Ezra Pound fulminating the various enterprises, the little magazines, the fugitive manifestos that constituted early Modernism first in South Kensington and then on the Left Bank; of the young Robert Bly, a Harvard graduate holed up at his farm on the plains of Minnesota, rallying the forces of the Midwestern "deep image" school of James Wright, Galway Kinnell, Donald Hall. Pound, whose early poetry is still his lasting achievement in my view, had seriously lost focus during his last years in London and Paris, and only gained it again when he moved to Italy and poured his awe-inspiring energies into the composition of the *Cantos.* Many readers of Bly would feel that his poetry has, over the years, taken second place to his work in the "new man" movement and to his activities as a performer of his own work.

Wheatley is still in the process of finding his way. There is a brittleness, a tentative and emotionally veiled quality to his poems that reminds me both of the English poet Michael Hofmann and of the early Paul Muldoon. Like Muldoon he is an accomplished rhymer, an extraordinarily rare quality in this day and age. Wheatley's skill shows itself to advantage in 'Autumn, the

Nightwalk, the City, the River'. Dublin, like London and Paris, is drenched in literary associations, and it is good to see an update that avoids the obvious. Here are a few lines from the middle of the poem with its crisp, satisfying couplets:

> Anywhere would do: I remember suburbs
> plush with hatchbacks parked on tidy kerbs,
> privets, cherry blossoms, nouveau riches'
> houses named for saints, complete with cable dishes;
> and then the streets where every window has
> an iron grid across its pane of glass,
> the garden weeds in cracks, a noise ahead—
> a bird, a car—enough to make me cross the road.

Another Dublin poem, 'Misery Hill', seizes on the evocative street-name, captures the atmosphere of urban decay which is not hard to find in the city, but does not rise above undifferentiated irony:

> a post-office van
> passes silently by with letters
> for anywhere but this grim street
> with its rubble and wire-topped walls,
> featureless and empty besides.

More daring and kinetic is Wheatley's *jeu d'esprit* 'St. John and the Eagle', based on illuminations executed for the gospel of John from the medieval Lindisfarne Gospels. The saint's emblematic eagle lifts right off the illuminated page in this brilliantly self-consuming poem, and onto the page of the poem:

> the eagle will swoop,
> scattering doves as he goes.
> Evangelist's bird, tired
> of the easy kill, the flocculent hare
>
> and deckchair legs of the deer
> folding under a ton's worth of rapt
> persuasion in its claw; from a thousand
> yards up the eagle has spied

and will snatch from your hands
your book, leaving you only
a feather with which to scatter
and sow the Word in his

fugitive image, imago aquilae:
no sooner will you have finished
this page than talons will
punctuate and carry it off.

Earlier, I made a comparison between Wheatley and Paul Muldoon. Like the young Muldoon, Wheatley is curious and ranges widely in search of poetic models. I enjoy seeing his poetic experiments that have appeared in literary magazines since this anthology was published. For example, two poems in the autumn 2005 *Poetry Ireland Review*, 'An Errancy' and 'Drift', play off traditional models from Irish folklore and Gaelic poetry with a welcome playfulness and emotional accessibility often lacking in the selections in the Wake Forest anthology.

Parenthetically, the efforts of Yeats, MacNeice, Heaney and—in his idiosyncratic and oblique way—Kavanagh, to define the Irish nation in its early years must seem largely the work of the past to the poets in the Wake Forest anthology. But this is not to say that they would agree with Margaret Thatcher that "there is no such thing as society". Clifton's short poem, 'Military Presence, Cobh 1899' obliquely addresses British colonialism in Ireland; the poem's terse ending—"all you lack / Is consciousness, judgement, the twentieth century"—suggests that Irish independence is less a matter of heroism than of historical inevitability. This would ruffle a few feathers. O'Driscoll's 'Them and You' points to the presence of a class structure in Ireland unforeseen by the 1916 visionaries.

Wheatley's social awareness would seem to attach, at least in these poems, more to the city of Dublin than to the country of Ireland. Derek Mahon in *The Yellow Book* has chronicled the metamorphosis of the city into "a Georgian theme-park for the tourist", "aliens, space invaders clicking at the front door, / goofy in baseball caps and nylon leisurewear", in a Dublin where "foreign investment conspires against old decency, / computer talks to computer, machine to answering machine". In a sonnet sequence addressed to the 19th-century poet James Clarence Mangan, Wheatley writes even more caustically:

> Let the city sleep on undisturbed,
> new hotels and apartment blocks replace
> the Dublin that we brick by brick erase;
> let your city die without a word
> of pity, indignation, grief or blame,
> the vampire crime lords fatten on its flesh
> and planners zone the corpse for laundered cash.

Sinéad Morrissey, who was born in Armagh and grew up in Belfast, bears witness to urban destruction brought on not by prosperity, corruption and "progress" but by bombs. In a startling little poem she personifies the Europa Hotel, a landmark in downtown Belfast which used regularly to be targeted by IRA bombers:

> It's a hard truth to have to take in the face—
> You wake up one morning with your windows
> Round your ankles and your forehead billowing smoke;
> Your view impaired for another fortnight
> Of the green hills they shatter you for.

The last lines briskly anatomise the ironies of the IRA campaign.

The first fifteen pages of the thirty-odd pages devoted to Morrissey make it blindingly clear that we are in the presence of a new talent whose "new angels" as she puts it, "are howling, hard", sandpapery, open-hearted. Work of this order renews one's faith in the art of poetry. 'Sea Stones' is a poem one is unlikely to forget. This brilliant study of the experience of receiving violence, of the complications of jealousy, of the unfathomable labyrinths of love and passion, begins,

> It is exactly a year today since you slapped me in public.
> I took it standing up. You claimed I just ignored it,
>   that I pretended to be hooked on the dumb-show of a
>   sunset,
>   splashing, a mile off. Too hooked to register
>   the sting of your ring finger
>   as it caught on my mouth and brought my skin with it.

I'll pass over an intermediate stanza and quote the ending of this poem that almost in itself is worth the price of the anthology. It is both deeply romantic and at the same time informed by a sense of human deviousness:

> He gave me roses. The surprise of butterflies caged in the
>   palms.
> And sea stones with tracings of juvenile kisses, scented with
>   risk.
> I wrapped them in black at the back of a bottom drawer,
> hidden in underwear. The truth—that you never were so vivid
>
> or so huge as the second the street turned towards us
> in shock—got dropped between us like a fallen match.
>
> You turned away as the sun disappeared like a ship. And I,
> Suddenly wanting to be struck again, to keep the fire of your
>   anger lit,
> I bit my lip.

The companion piece to this is '& Forgive Us Our Trespasses', which begins, "Of which the first is love". I leave this one to the reader to discover. Morrissey is an astute student of the human heart.

To an American, it is always interesting to see what a writer from another country makes of the US. Harry Clifton's 'Absinthe at New Orleans' combines vivid sketches of American cityscapes with some trenchant criticism of social inequalities in the United States; at the same time the poem is informed by bizarre Kafkaesque fantasies of the State Department agency that is paying for his tour of the US as a sinister, all-seeing Big Brother pulling strings behind the scenes. One can only wonder what this otherwise seemingly sensible poet had been smoking. Sinéad Morrissey takes a less ideologically motivated view of our country. I like her American landscapes:

> From the window of the midnight-bound Vegas plane
> Tucson flares in the desert—a cactus pricked by rain;
> lit houses, lit highways and floodlit swimming pools—
> a stunned bird in a basin, spreading its wings to cool.

Her extraordinary poem, 'An Anatomy of Smell', contains a portrait of a couple, one American from the Southwest, one Irish, rendered in terms of smell:

> From you, the smell of the Tucson desert:
> copper deposits, animal skulls, the chalk trajectory
> of stars no cloud covers or strains, ochre and chilli.
> From me, bog cotton, coal fires, wild garlic, river dirt.
> And from the two of us, salt. When we move house
> such genealogies as these will follow us.

I don't own Morrissey's two books, *There Was Fire in Vancouver,* 1996, and *Between Here and There,* 2002, but I am guessing that the first poems of her selections in the anthology are from the earlier book and the latter poems from the second. To me the earlier poems speak more convincingly. The later ones would appear to grow out of travel to places like Japan, New York, New Zealand—places that are not as evocative for this poet as those about the American Southwest or her emotional home places. The meditations on history, the poem about whales off the Ulster coast, all of these strike one as "occasional" poems. Except for 'Genetics', a haunting exploration of how a separated mother and father have left their legacy in their daughter's hands—"My father's in my fingers, but my mother's in my palms"—they lack the rough edge of necessity.

Caitríona O'Reilly, just a year younger than Sinéad Morrissey, is an accomplished young poet who is struggling, I feel, to emerge from the complications of the many things she can do well. She's like a woman with seventeen pieces of expensive luggage who can't find the perfect "little black dress" that is folded away somewhere. Look how well, in 'Fragment', she does the Plath-influenced ominous landscape:

> This night-breathing deceives, it is so calm,
> The headland glitters with beached faces, lunar stares,
> a tidal moon-haul of wrecks and drownings.
> Their gazes are blank and lasting,
> outfacing constellations even, crystalline.

The first of her 'Two Night Time Pieces' called 'Pisces', is a place where something vital and not at all impersonal or mortifying tries and succeeds in making itself felt through a scaffolding of perceptions that are perhaps so precise and "poetic" that they actually get in the way. This very sexy poem made me gasp with pleasure and interrupt the person who was reading beside me in bed, to insist she hear it read aloud:

> Thirteen Februaries slept through
> before I learned what going under meant.
>
> Pale and thin as sheets,
> the near fields burst free of mooring.
>
> Then the turn of the tide,
> the sea stack,
>
> the pier-light's onyx eye.
> Those teenage dreams
>
> were cuttle-ink tattoos
> describing blue-rinse mermen,
>
> each muscular wave awash
> with sex and phosphor.

I was awash and rocked,
rocked hard to wake

and woke, drenched to the roots,
my flannelette pyjamas stiff with sand.

"Blue-rinse mermen" is overly fussy, and I even have my doubts about "cuttle-ink tattoos", which is *recherché* in a manner reminiscent of Marianne Moore. But the assonance, the repetitions, the wood-block tones of "awash and rocked, / rocked hard to wake // and woke, drenched to the roots" are thrilling. And the domestically diminutive, adolescent note introduced by "flannelette pyjamas" reminds me, in its rightness, of Leonard Cohen's line in 'Back on Boogie Street' from *Ten New Songs:* "I've tidied up the kitchenette, / I've tuned the old banjo".

A beautiful example of transformation is O'Reilly's suite of poems, 'A Quartet for the Falcon', based, I should think, on her readings in falconry and alchemy. Perhaps she has just made it all up and made it sounds plausible. Here is a peregrine falcon hunting a heron:

They go ringing up the air,
each in its separate spiral stair
to the indigo rim of the skies,
            then descend
      swift as a murderer's hand
with a knife. Death's gesture liquefies

in bringing the priestly heron down.
Her prize, the marrow from a wing-bone
in which she delights, her spurred
            fleur-de-lys tongue
      stained gold-vermilion—
little angel in her hangman's hood.

I believe that Caitríona O'Reilly is on her way to becoming a stunning lyric poet. She is not the first poet to have earned a PhD, not will she be the last. But a way must be found to transmute all the learning into lore, in the way Ezra Pound did in his early poetry and then forgot how to do through most of the *Cantos*.

The Wake Forest series, originally under the guidance of Dillon Johnston, has always been a pioneer—almost *the* pioneer—in introducing new Irish poetry to American readers. It will be interesting to see which poets the press decides to present next. Ireland's standing army of poets is as numerous as ever, so there will be no lack of choices. A note of caution about the cross-fertilisation between American and Irish poetry might not be out of place. Jefferson Holdridge closes his thirty-page introduction to this volume with a couple of sentences that I found chilling: "Poetry is ridding itself of everything that is not concerned with poetic perception, impersonal and mortifying. Caitríona O'Reilly's efforts to look at the changing world with new eyes are ambitious, even historic, at this pivotal period in Ireland". My own view is that if it rids itself of everything that is not concerned with poetic perception, poetry isolates itself in ways that are damaging both to its potential readership and to its very essence. Two adjectives float at the end of the sentence I have quoted, so it is hard to be sure what they modify, but presumably Mr Holdridge is praising a poetic vision that is impersonal and mortifying. "Impersonal" works if applied to, say, Dennis O'Driscoll's poems which by-pass the self in order to be what Matthew Arnold called "a criticism of life". But "mortifying"? Does one read poetry in order to be mortified? I don't. But no doubt I am being unfair to the editor of this collection.

What concerns me here is that American poetry has lost much of its traditional readership in the years during which poets have found a home in academia. Only in such an atmosphere could a sentence such as "Poetry is ridding itself of everything that is not concerned with poetic perception, impersonal and mortifying" be written or credited. By contrast, despite the inroads that television, computer games, iPods and so forth have made into literacy, poetry has retained its centrality within the Irish national culture. On the one hand Irish-language poetry continues to flourish. Nuala Ní Dhomhnaill's work is read both in the original and in translations from poets as adept as Paul Muldoon. Gabriel Rosenstock's enthusiasm for haiku has attracted much notice, as have the revitalizing results Cathal Ó Searcaigh has achieved by translating the spirit of the Beats into Irish.

In English, Eiléan Ní Chuilleanáin has quietly followed her own path to become a major poet. Paul Durcan, Tony Curtis, Paula Meehan and Brendan Kennelly have provided Ireland with genuinely popular poets the likes of which one looks for in vain in the US. All over the country, poetry continues to find "a local habitation and a name". The struggling little town of Carrick-on-Suir in Tipperary has found its poetic champion in Michael Coady, as have Galway and Connemara in the poems of Mary O'Malley. Cork has found a voice for its unique culture—closer in some ways to continental Europe than to these islands—not only in Ní Chuilleanáin but even more fully in the work of Thomas McCarthy. Desmond O'Grady, from his redoubt in Kinsale, has for years lived in a Mediterranean of the mind and soul. Peter Sirr is just as European in outlook as Harry Clifton. And whose voice and body of experience could surprise readers of Seamus Heaney's poetry from abroad as much as Leland Bardwell's? Poets like Macdara Woods have taken to performing live with musicians, providing evenings of very refined entertainment for those who enjoy a blending of the two art forms. Immigrants such as Mark Roper and James Harpur have become so naturalized here that one would think twice before calling them anything but Irish.

And then there are the contributions made by Irish writers like Eamonn Wall, Greg Delanty, Eavan Boland and Eamon Grennan who have emigrated to America, and Bernard O'Donoghue and Matthew Sweeney who reside in the UK, but still live in a country of the imagination clearly identifiable as Ireland. I could mention many other poets to support the case for diversity on the Irish poetry scene, such as Thomas Lynch, who oscillates back and forth between Michigan and West Clare. Theo Dorgan, through his work in broadcasting, has brought a poet's sensibility to the public domain, as have Peter Fallon and Pat Boran in the world of publishing. My point is that where a broad spectrum of people read poetry, an audience exists for a great variety of approaches. I hope Irish poetry will continue to resist the increasing professionalism of its American counterpart.

An earlier version of 'The Future of Irish Poetry?' was originally published in *Poetry Ireland Review*, #89, March 2007. The essay was later featured on the website, *Poetry Daily*, for 22 May 2007, and published as a chapter in *Finding Ireland: a Poet's Explorations of Irish Literature and Culture*, by Richard Tillinghast, University of Notre Dame Press, 2008.

NOTES ON CONTRIBUTORS

EAVAN BOLAND was born in Dublin in 1944 and studied in Ireland, London and New York. She has taught at Trinity College, Dublin, University College, Dublin, and Bowdoin College, Maine; she was also a member of the International Writing Program at the University of Iowa. She is currently Mabury Knapp Professor in the Humanities at Stanford University, California. A pioneering figure in Irish poetry, she is widely published on both sides of the Atlantic. Her collections include *Night Feed* (1982/1994), *The Journey* (1987), *The Lost Land* (1998), *Code* (2001) and *Domestic Violence* (2007). *An Origin Like Water: Collected Poems* was published in 1996. *Object Lessons* (1995) is a collection of her prose writings. She has also edited, with Mark Strand, *A Norton Anthology of Poetic Forms* (2000). Her awards include a Lannan Foundation Award in Poetry and an American Ireland Fund Literary Award. She divides her time between California and Dublin where she lives with her husband, the novelist Kevin Casey.

PAT BORAN was born in Portlaoise in 1963 and has long since lived in Dublin where he has worked as a radio broadcaster, literature festival organiser and, more recently, as editor of the Dedalus Press. The recipient of the 1989 Patrick Kavanagh Award for Poetry, he has published four full-length collections of poetry, and his *New and Selected Poems* was published by Salt Publishing in the UK in 2005 and reissued by Dedalus Press in 2007. His writing for children includes the Bisto Book of the Year Award finalist, *All the Way from China* (1998). Prose works include the popular writing handbook, *The Portable Creative Writing Workshop* (1999, reissued 2005). He has edited *Wingspan: A Dedalus Sampler* (2006) and is a former editor of *Poetry Ireland Review*. He received the 2008 Lawrence O'Shaughnessy Award for Irish Poetry and is a member of Aosdána.

CIARAN CARSON was born in 1948 and lives in his native Belfast. From 1975 to 1998 he worked for the Arts Council of Northern Ireland, with responsibility for Traditional Music, and, latterly, Literature, and in 2003 he was appointed Professor of Poetry and Director of the Seamus Heaney Centre at Queen's University. He is the author of eleven collections of poems, including *Collected Poems* (2008), and four highly-praised prose works. Among his many prizes and awards are the Irish Times Literature Prize, the T.S. Eliot Prize, the Oxford Weidenfeld Translation Prize (for *Dante's Inferno*, 2002) and the 2003 Forward Prize. He is a member of Aosdána.

THEO DORGAN was born in Cork in 1953 and lives in Dublin where he has been Director of Poetry Ireland and has worked extensively as a broadcaster of literary programmes on both radio and television. He has published three volumes of poems, the first two of which, *The Ordinary House of Love* (1991) and *Rosa Mundi* (1995) were reissued in a single volume, *What This Earth Cost Us*, by the Dedalus Press in 2008. His work has appeared in translation in Spanish and Italian. Together with Gene Lambert he edited *The Great Book of Ireland* (1991); with Noel Duffy, *Watching the River Flow* (Poetry Ireland / Éigse Éireann, 1999); and with Malcolm Maclean, *An Leabhar Mòr / The Great Book of Gaelic* (2002). *Sailing for Home*, his account of a voyage from Antigua to Kinsale was one of the most admired Irish books of 2004. He edited *The Book of Uncommon Prayer* (2007). He was a member of The Arts Council / An Chomhairle Ealaíon from 2003 to 2008. He is a member of Aosdána.

EAMON GRENNAN was born in Dublin in 1941. His most recent poetry collections, published by Gallery Press in Ireland, and by Graywolf Press in the U.S. are *Still Life with Waterfall* (which won the Lenore Marshall Award), *The Quick of It*, and *Out of Breath* (the American edition of which, enlarged, is called *Matter of Fact*), as well as a co-translation (with Rachel Kitzinger) of *Oedipus at Colonus*, published by Oxford University Press. His volume of criticism, *Facing the Music: Irish Poetry in the 20th Century*, appeared in 1999. He taught for many years in the English Department of Vassar College, and now teaches occasionally in the graduate writing programs of Columbia University and NYU. He divides his time between Poughkeepsie and the West of Ireland.

SEAMUS HEANEY was born in County Derry in 1939 and now lives in Dublin. He taught English and poetry at Queen's University, Belfast, and at Harvard University, and was professor of poetry at Oxford University from 1989 to 1994. His many volumes of poetry, criticism and translations have established him as one of the leading poets of his generation. His many awards and honours include the Whitbread Book of the Year, on two occasions (for *The Spirit Level*, 1996, and *Beowulf*, 1999), the T.S. Eliot Prize (for *District and Circle*, 2007), and the Nobel Prize for Literature in 1995. He was elected Saoi of Aosdána in 1997.

THOMAS KINSELLA was born in Dublin in 1928 and, after university, entered the Civil Service before becoming a full-time writer and teacher in the United States. He is the author of over thirty collections of poetry, and has translated extensively from the Irish, notably the great epic *The Táin*. He was a director of the Dolmen Press and Cuala Press, and in 1972 founded the Peppercanister Press for the publication of sequences and long occasional poems which now appear jointly through the Dedalus Press in Ireland and Carcanet Press in the UK. He is the editor of *The New Oxford Book of Irish Verse* and of Austin Clarke's *Selected Poems* and *Collected Poems*. He is also the author of *The Dual Tradition*, a critical essay on poetry and politics in Ireland. His many awards and honours include Guggenheim Fellowships, the Denis Devlin Memorial Award, the Arts Council Triennial Book Award and honorary doctorates from the University of Turin and the National University of Ireland. Together with the artist Louis Le Brocquy he was awarded the Freedom of the City of Dublin in 2007. *A Dublin Documentary* is a collection of poems, reminiscences and photographs (O'Brien Press, 2006).

MICHAEL LONGLEY was born in Belfast in 1939, and was educated at the Royal Belfast Academical Institution and Trinity College, Dublin. He worked as a teacher, and served as director of literature and traditional arts for the Arts Council of Northern Ireland from 1970 to 1991. His many books of poetry include *No Continuing City* (1969), *An Exploded View* (1973), *Man Lying on a Wall* (1976), *The Echo Gate* (1979), *The Ghost Orchid* (1995), short-listed for the T.S. Eliot Award. *Gorse Fires* won the Whitbread Poetry Prize in 1991, and *The Weather in Japan* won the Irish Times Literature Prize for Poetry, the Hawthornden Prize and the T.S. Eliot Prize in 2001. An autobiographical work, *Tuppeny Stung*, appeared in 1994, and he has edited selections of poems by Louis MacNeice and W. R. Rodgers. Other awards include the Irish-American Cultural Institute Award and the Eric Gregory Award, which he shared with Derek Mahon in 1965. In 2001, he was awarded the Queen's Gold Medal for Poetry. He is a fellow of the Royal Society of Literature, and lives in Belfast. His *Collected Poems* was published in 2007.

JOHN MONTAGUE was born in Brooklyn, New York, in 1929, was raised in Co. Tyrone, and educated at University College Dublin, and Yale University and the University of California at Berkeley. A co-founder of Claddagh Records, he became president of Poetry Ireland in 1979. He has taught at UCD, University College Cork, the Sorbonne, and at several American universities. His volumes of poetry include *Forms of Exile* (1958), *Poisoned Lands* (1961), *A Chosen Light* (1967), *The Rough Field* (1972), which was performed with music by the Chieftains at the Peacock Theatre, *A Slow Dance* (1975), *The Great Cloak* (1978), *The Dead Kingdom* (1984), *Mount Eagle* (1988), *Time in Armagh* (1993), *Collected Poems* (1995), *Smashing the Piano* (1999) and *Drunken Sailor* (2004). He published *Carnac*, a translation of work by the French poet Guillevic, in 1999. *The*

Lost Notebook, a novella based on his youthful years in Florence, won the first Hughes Award in 1987 and he has since published two volumes of memoir, *Company* (2001) and *The Pear is Ripe* (2007). Among the anthologies he has edited are *The Faber Book of Irish Verse* (1974) and *Bitter Harvest: An Anthology of Irish Poetry* (1989). His many awards and honours include the Marten Toonder Award in 1977, a Guggenheim fellowship in 1980, and the Ireland Funds Literary Award in 1995. He was the inaugural Ireland Professor of Poetry from 1998 to 2001. He is a member of Aosdána.

EILÉAN NÍ CHUILLEANÁIN was born in Cork in 1942, and studied at University College Cork, and at Oxford University. Her collections of poetry include *Acts and Monuments* (1972), which won the Patrick Kavanagh Award in 1973, *Site of Ambush* (1975), *The Second Voyage* (1977), *The Rose Geranium* (1981), *The Magdalene Sermons* (1989), nominated for the European Literature Prize in 1992, *The Brazen Serpent* (1994), *The Girl Who Married the Reindeer* (2001) and *Selected Poems* (2008). She won the O'Shaughnessy Prize for Poetry from the Irish-American Cultural Institute in 1992. In 1975 she co-founded Cyphers, a literary magazine, with Pearse Hutchinson, Macdara Woods and Leland Bardwell. She is a fellow of Trinity College, Dublin, where she has taught English since 1966; she also teaches on courses in literary translation and comparative literature. She has translated poetry from several languages, including, with Medbh McGuckian, The Water Horse from the Irish of Nuala Ní Dhomhnaill; with Cormac Ó Cuilleanáin, Verbale/Minutes/Tuairisc from the Italian of Michele Ranchetti; and *After the Raising of Lazarus* from the Romanian of Ileana Malancioiu. Married to the poet Macdara Woods, Eileán Ní Chillleanáin divides her times between Dublin and Umbria. She is a member of Aosdána.

NUALA NÍ DHOMHNAILL was born in Lancashire in 1952 to Irish parents, she was brought up in the Dingle Gaeltacht and in Nenagh, Co. Tipperary, and was educated at University College, Cork. Her collections of poetry include *An Dealg Droighin* (1981), *Féar Suaithinseach* (1984), *Rogha Dánta / Selected Poems* (1986, 1988, 1990), *Pharaoh's Daughter* (1990), *Feis* (1991), *The Astrakhan Cloak* (1992), *Spíonáin is Róiseanna* (1993), *In the Heart of Europe: Poems for Bosnia* (1998) and *Cead Aighnis* (2000). *The Water Horse* appeared with translations by Medbh McGuckian and Eiléan Ní Chuilleanáin in 1999, and her work has also frequently been translated by Michael Hartnett, Seamus Heaney, Paul Muldoon and Michael Longley. In 1995, she edited *Jumping off Shadows: Selected Contemporary Irish Poets* with Greg Delanty, and she has written several children's plays. She

received Duais Sheáin Uí Ríordáin in 1982, 1984 and 1990, Duais Na
Chomhairle Ealaíne um Filíochta in 1985 and 1988, Gradam an
Oireachtais (1984), the Irish American Foundation O'Shaughnessy Award
for Poetry (1988), and the American Ireland Fund Literature Prize (1991).
She was writer in residence for Dún Laoghaire Rathdown County Council
in 1998, and she taught at New York University, Boston College and
Villanova University in the U.S. In 2001 she became Ireland Professor of
Poetry. She lives in Dublin.

BERNARD O'DONOGHUE was born in Co. Cork in 1945 and moved to
Manchester, England when he was 16, where he attended St Bede's
College. He has lived in Oxford since 1965 and is currently fellow and
tutor in Old English and Medieval English, Linguistics and the History of
the English Language at Wadham College, Oxford University. He was
previously Reader at Magdalen College, Oxford. His poetry collections
include *Poaching Rights* (1987), *The Absent Signifier* (1990), *The Weakness*
(1991), *Gunpowder* (1995), which won the Whitbread Prize for Poetry,
Here Nor There (1999), *Poaching Rights* (1999), *Outliving* (2003) and
Selected Poems (2008). In 2006, Penguin Books published his translation of
Sir Gawain and the Green Knight. He is a member of Aosdána. His critical
writing includes *The Courtly Love Tradition* (1984), *Seamus Heaney and the
Language of Poetry* (1995) and *Oxford Irish Quotations* (1999). He is a
member of Aosdána.

CATHAL Ó SEARCAIGH was born in Donegal in 1956, and lives at the foot
of Mount Errigal. His many volumes of poetry include *Miontraigéide
Cathrach* (1975), *Tuirlingt* (1979), *Súile Shuibhne* (1983), *Suibhne* (1987),
An Bealach na Bhaile (1990), *Homecoming* (1993), *Na Buachaillí Bána*
(1995) and *Out in the Open* (1997). His selected poems, *Ag Tnúth leis an
tSolas: 1975-2000,* won the Irish Times' Irish language literature prize in
2001. More recently he published *Caiseal na gCorr: Poems and Photographs*
(2002), *Seal in Neipeal* (2003), an account of his travels in Nepal and his
most recent poetry collection, *Gúru i gClúidíní,* in 2006. Selections of his
work have been translated into French, Breton, Italian, German, Russian,
Danish and Japanese, and have also been set to music. He won the Seán Ó
Riordáin Prize for Poetry in 1994 and the Duais Bhord na Gaeilge in 1995.
His memoir, Light on Distant Mountains, will be published this year by
Simon & Schuster. He is a member of Aosdána.

RICHARD TILLINGHAST was born in 1940 in Memphis, Tennessee. He came
to Kinvara, County Galway, for a year in 1990 on an Amy Lowell Travel
Grant and has long since been a distinctive presence on the Irish literary

scene: his new and selected poems, *Today in the Café Trieste,* appeared from Salmon Publishing in 1997 and he has also been a Director of The Poets' House in Co. Donegal; his most recent pubication is *Finding Ireland: a Poet's Explorations of Irish Literature and Culture* (2008). In 2005 he retired from the faculty of the Master of Fine Arts program at the University of Michigan, where he had worked since the program's inception in 1983, and now lives in Co. Tipperary. He is the author of eight books of poetry, most recently *The New Life* (Copper Beech Press, 2008). He has also published three books of essays including *Robert Lowell's Life and Work: Damaged Grandeur* (University of Michigan Press, 1995). In collaboration with his daughter, Julia Clare Tillinghast, he is publishing *Dirty August,* a selection of poems translated from the Turkish poet Edip Cansever (Talisman Editions, 2009). Dedalus will publish his *Selected Poems* in 2009.

DAVID WHEATLEY was born in Dublin in 1970 and studied at Trinity College, Dublin. He is the author of three collections of poetry with Gallery Press: *Thirst* (1997), *Misery Hill* (2000), and *Mocker* (2006). He was a founding editor of the poetry journal Metre, and has edited the poetry of James Clarence Mangan. His criticism has appeared in many journals, including *London Review of Books, Times Literary Supplement, The Guardian* and *The Irish Times.* He has been a winner of the Friends Provident National Poetry Competition, the Rooney Prize for Irish Literature, and the Vincent Buckley Prize. He lectures at the University of Hull.

INDEX OF POETS

Dedalus Press
Poetry from Ireland and the world

Established in 1985, the Dedalus Press is one of Ireland's best-known literary imprints, dedicated to new Irish poetry and to poetry from around the world in English translation.

For further information on Dedalus Press titles, or to visit our Audio Room of free-to-download recordings by many of the poets on our list, see **www.dedaluspress.com**

Printed in the United States
146373LV00001B/5/P